Holding Patterns

Holding Patterns

Essays by A.F. Cannon

BONFIRE BOOKS

Holding Patterns

Published 2022 by Bonfire Books: Melbourne, Australia.

© 2022 Alasdair Cannon

ISBN: 978-0-6450664-7-0

Bonfire Books
<u>bonfirebooks.org</u>

Cover: Lily Hull

With thanks to Jason Beer

Contents

Foreword

This book, *Holding Patterns*, is a collection of words about language, politics, and culture. It contains six essays, all written between September 2020 and May 2021.

The essays cover an array of topics—workplace bullying and Obama's presidency, Beckett's novels and Nintendo games, 9/11 and mass media, the Freudian theory of melancholia and modern labour markets, etc. Yet their variety belies their consistent focus: the patterns of emotion, language, belief, and action that make up our lives and relationships.

Holding Patterns was written to describe our more traumatic loops of behaviour, to find their origins, and ultimately to break them: it seeks the lines of flight that might lead us to other skies, to more graceful ways of passing through the air.

For this reason, *Holding Patterns* is a book of faith and hope, created with the belief that language can both confine and free, and with the hope that words can liberate us from the repeated spirals that leave us less human and alive over time.

Alasdair Cannon, Brisbane, March 2022

Some Notes on What She May Know as 'Empathy'
Reflections for R U OK? Day 2020.

I
R U OK? DAY, 2019

I HAVE THIS MEMORY. The sun burns, a golden glow clambering slantwise through the room. We all stand, waiting to hear her words. It is September 11th, 2019. Trays of relatively edible hors d'oeuvres decay on round, high tables. Compassionate black-and-gold posters adorn the border of the room. In the air, silence and exhalations: the inorganic suspiring of a quiet corporate office. The diaphragmatic expansions of people who have attended subsidised psychotherapy.

She takes a breath. Palpable vulnerability. 'Okay,' she says. 'The décor has given away the surprise: today is R U OK? Day. And this means we're going to talk about mental health. About listening. Empathy.' A discourse on the dark and the light; the chiaroscuro of the human heart.

As she speaks, I fade from the world into my own thoughts. Unconsciously I take a handful of unnameable savoury things from a bowl next to me. The strange signs of high society: some of these snacks were a familiar shade of 20mg Brintellix red.[1]

---

[1] Vortioxetine tablets manufactured by H. Lundbeck A/S. An SSRI used to treat MDD, GAD and other mood disorders, it comes in four doses and three colours: pink for 5mg and 15mg; yellow for those on a 10mg dose; and red if you take 20mg. Also

Carmine, incarnadine, almond-shaped like mother's eyes. I put them in my mouth and swallow. A shadow of the cardinal art I had rehearsed by lamplight each night for three years. Tip the head up, blood to the back of the skull, expose the throat, try not to choke.

Ordinarily I have disdain for corporate initiatives where profiteering masquerades as tender care. R U OK? Day, however, is an exception. I suffer from recurrent anxiety and depression. The eternal return; again and again, my pain resurfaces. I knew I would be compelled to tell them about my suffering soon. My violent delights with violent ends. To say, with sad language, that I was not okay. Fearing the exposure that comes with confession, I was happy that my boss showed us she cared. I had moved cities for this job. Left friends behind. I had worked as her graduate assistant for three weeks, and her words made me think and hope I was less alone.

Hope: that's where my recollection ends. With a hope that I wouldn't feel isolated there. With a hope I could speak if necessary. With a hope that, this time, I would be okay.

I believe I have this memory. I really feel the flood of the sun, the rush of comfort. It's all there in pieces, in glittering splinters. But in truth, I might be confusing things. It's difficult to say. My memory of my time at the organisation isn't fantastic. A common symptom of depression, stress and anxiety, you see, is mnemonic decline: an inability to piece together the impressions of your past into a coherent whole. To make sense. For the depressed, the yellow burst of our days, the heat of our words, the quiet drip of time—these blur together, making a mad slag of molten gold that casts our eyes askance in all directions. The depressive tries to catch the light; but he is blind. And as I worked for my boss, I soon lost my sight once again.

---

known as Trintellix in some foreign markets, namely the USA, where the name was changed to avoid confusion with the Ticagrelor tablet, Brilinta® of AstraZeneca PLC, the pharmaceutical and biopharmaceutical company responsible for making a promising COVID-19 vaccine.

II
NOT OK

Despite the support I felt that day, only six months passed before I quit. Once again, I spiralled into mental illness: the schizoid retreat with its frantic language, the panicked anguish that ends with the death-draw.

(One more time with feeling.)

Throughout my life, my depression has ostensibly arrived without cause. My sadness was never a counterpoint to anything specific. Nor was it a harmonic moment of an emotional melody. It just *was*. I thought it was metaphysical, ontological. The doctors told me it was biological; neurochemistry gone awry. I was serotonergically deprived, drained of dopamine, they said. The pain and the torpor were nobody's fault. I thought I knew the deal.

Yet this time was different. Blinded by rationalisations, it took me too long to realise that my symptoms sprung neither from my body nor spirit. They were not the signs of an isolated mind. No: now I was pushed to despair by my boss's behaviour. My sadness came from my relations, and not from nothing.

My boss, a person in her early 60s, was the director of our organisation. I met her on my first day at the company. I found her charming if a little saccharine. She said we would work closely together, so I would need to understand the 'crazy world' inside her mind. A person with a literary sensibility, this early meeting established all the major themes of our relationship— deception, insanity, and authority—and augured her behaviour in the months to come.

The sweetness that belied her vicious underside quickly dissolved after our first encounter. Her false persona began to lapse. I saw tactless[2] moments of dismissal and unkindness: sadistic slips and quick, violent flickers in her eyes. Flashes of otherness would emerge between her words, only to recede immediately, like a light that rises from the depths of a lake and

---

[2]   Or calculated.

is then drawn backwards, vanishing, while its traces shimmer upon the water's veneer. Fleeting impressions of disturbing significance, only just hidden, would appear and then they were gone, retreating back beyond the limits of articulation. Her affability was the obverse of a refined, hidden sadism, and like everything we try to hide, these seemingly minor elements of her personality eventually proved decisive. Soon they dominated our interactions and filled the space between us.

Every week she would request new work of me in a vague and ambiguous email or during a rambling and baffling meeting. This work was sometimes completely outside my area of expertise, demanding skills of me that were not in the job description and which I did not have. Usually though it was just far below my skill level, and this was because she couldn't yet trust me: I was new, you see, and I needed the training they promised to provide later. Determined to prove that I was not worthy of trust or more challenging work, my boss never offered this training to me, and said that everything I completed was wrong. 'Not good enough,' she would say. 'Do it again.' So I would say, 'Okay,' and I would do it again. But by the time I had revised the work, her goals, never entirely clear to me, had changed. Different things were needed. She would discard or ignore the previous work and send me off with new instructions even more baffling than the last. And then the cycle would repeat, the tension rising every round.

My boss had a litany of excuses for this behaviour. She couldn't pay attention to my work because her medical treatments made her feel unwell. She spoke over me and disregarded my opinions because, being a woman, people never listened to her. 'Oh,' I would say. 'I'm so sorry. I hope you're okay.' At the same time, she was creative when condemning me. Where I failed to understand her, I revealed my inability to take instructions. If she didn't comprehend something, I had poor communication skills.[3] 'Oh,' I would say. 'I'm so sorry. I'll do

---

[3]   Once, she forced me to spend three weeks making a PowerPoint presentation to improve my communication skills[a] after she

better next time.'

Quickly, things worsened. I learned that if I deviated from her instructions in any way, I would be criticised; I also learned that if I didn't try to add extra, useful things to my work that she hadn't requested, I would be condemned.

Terrified of being fired, my anxiety raged with a new ferocity. I went to see the organisation's in-house psychologist. R U OK? Day posters hung on the walls of their office as I completed a mental health questionnaire. I scored 39/40 on this suffering quiz. This meant my symptoms were 'severe.' This meant I was not ok. So we spoke about possible causes, and together we reified my pain, made it existential. 'My life does feel pretty meaningless,' I claimed. Deferring to the masculine panacea, I said I might start lifting weights to combat the void.

Though it is obvious now, it took me months to realise that her behaviour was the source of my suffering. And in this time where I blamed nothing for my pain, my life became unbearable. I started vomiting before work. Taking diazepam[4] to sleep. Stress fractures appeared in my teeth. Soon I was near-delirious with fatigue, and it was then that I noticed some dramatic ironies in my life. In my savage anxiety, I became excruciatingly aware of the fact that my job was funded by a charitable organisation whose endowment came from a private mental health care company; my father even held shares in that company. Funny, ha ha. And though it was months after the occasion, I noticed that R U OK? Day posters were still everywhere. In the coffee room, the bathrooms, the lifts: the crassly happy yellow-and-black signs

---

misunderstood a point made in a document that she misread. The information she needed was on the page but because I hadn't anticipated the fact that she would read the information out of order, I was in the wrong and had to be punished.

[a] Making the before-tax cost of this exercise something like $5,000 AUD.

[4] More commonly known as Valium, due to the wildly successful patent-protected variant that hit the market first. I take a generic brand, APO-Diazepam, 5mg, manufactured by Apotex Pty Ltd.

were all around, xanthic, lambent, ambient, beaming from the walls. The colour of madness, the colour of nothing.[5] With their strange mix of care and authority, they relentlessly questioned my mental health. In response, I could only quote Pulp Fiction's Marsellus Wallace. *Nah, man*, I thought. *I'm pretty fucking far from okay.*

Later, and on yet another day I quietly fantasised about dying, a woman joined me in the building's lift as I rode it to the ground. I had never seen her before. We said hello and she told me she was a senior staff member in my department. And then, apropos of nothing, she asked me if I liked working there. As she spoke, her eyes quivered slightly, brimming with what I saw as understanding. I don't know why she asked, but it may have been the way I carried myself. Lockjawed, defensive, perditionistic: despite the mind, the body communicates. And it's strange to say it, but her empathy shocked me. A symptom of starvation, a sign of kindness from another life. A silence followed, and both her and I knew she had cracked open my heart; my pain was obvious, and I didn't want to lie. Yet I told her I loved it, smiled, and stepped out of the lift. So much for honesty.

This lie proved decisive. In its wake, the noise in my heart erupted, and I realised that my workplace had become a contradiction. With the velocity and force of revelation, I became conscious of my suffering and its source: my boss was to blame. Yet even though we had reassuring talks on R U OK? Day in 2019, I had no desire to voice my concerns. My reasons were simple. My organisation offered support to those who suffered psychologically; yet it was directed by a person who took pains to produce such suffering in her employees. Their messaging was totally dissonant: ironic and cacophonous. Yet it seemed that nobody had anything to say on this inharmoniousness at the heart of the corporation. Either nobody else was dissatisfied or there was an unspoken commitment to quietude. More importantly, my boss was the highest authority within the organisation, and she was a hypocrite. All our suffering words would fall on her

---

[5]   According to Frida Kahlo.

ears, and I did not trust her at all. If I exposed my vulnerability, I felt my situation would only worsen. I couldn't trust in speech or communication; silence, in my eyes, was the safest option. The sane, of course, can only remain silent for so long. At some point, they must release those yellow flames scorching black the insides of their heart; they face a fatal conflagration otherwise. Afraid to speak, I chose the only other alternative. Emptied of hope, I handed in my resignation and I sealed my fate.

After I resigned, I decided I had nothing to lose so I spoke of my suffering. In this way, I quickly discovered I wasn't alone. At the organisation, commiseration was the unspoken word, and some had it even worse than me. For a senior employee, the boss's destructive and undermining behaviours were even more brutal. First, she gave him incoherent tasks and shredded the results in front of him. Then, once she had demolished his motivation, she demoted him. Perversely, the demotion brought him joy, for it meant he would no longer work with her. Another colleague told me he was learning a new language to widen his job prospects. He wanted to leave because of her, yet he had debts and responsibilities; he couldn't quit his job without an alternative. Though he searched widely, that alternative proved elusive. He told me was considering a job in Holland. He told me he was learning Dutch. Mostly pragmatic vocabulary: *neerslachtigheid, verdriet.* He was desperate to leave, I guess.

Through conversations like this, I learned there was an abundance of such stories. There had been a 150% turnover in the administrative staff in the last eighteen months. We were haemorrhaging senior staff because of my boss's cruelty and blindness. The quality of work had nosedived. She wouldn't make eye contact with certain people in meetings. Furtive whispers everywhere. Through these stories, I realised she had cultivated an atmosphere of dread. Diffused through the building and mingling with our thoughts, a bitter miasma clouded our speech. There was a sadness in the air that everyone understood but which none of us would articulate. Here, now, I put words to this despair. Because of this person, the place had become a petty tyranny: a bully had taken charge of the organisation.

In many countries, mine included, bullying is prohibited by law. Workplace abuse carries significant consequences, and some jurisdictions have made bullying a criminal offence. In Victoria, Australia, 'serious bullying,' which includes behaviours that drive another to suicide, carries a maximum sentence of ten years in prison. These are harsh punishments; their severity reflects the immense damage that bullies can and do inflict on their victims.

At law, definitions of bullying tend to cast a wide net. This is a good thing: bullies can be cruel in all sorts of subtle ways, and they can also be creative, finding vast, untapped reservoirs for their sadism. It is crucial that the law is flexible and widely applicable. Otherwise, it can fall behind the bleeding edge of bullying innovations.

The anti-bullying laws in my country use three criteria to define bullying actions, and they capture a wide variety of behaviour. To constitute a punishable offence, a bully's actions must be a) repeated, b) unreasonable, and c) create a risk to health and safety.[6] According to the Fair Work Commission, all sorts of belittling, undermining and abusive behaviour can qualify. Intimidating your employees or giving them work below or outside their level of competence are typical examples of bullying behaviour. Berating them for failing to understand your own incomprehensible emails—maybe, that's another one. Ignoring or destroying their work that you demanded probably counts too. Really, there is a litany of possibilities. So long as there is a pattern of behaviour that a reasonable person would disavow, it can count as bullying.

An important aspect of our bullying laws is point c) of the definition: the need for the victim to prove that the behaviour could cause harm. The critical word here is 'could': fortunately for the subjects of bullying, actual harm is unnecessary, and things like anxiety, depression, sleep disturbances, nausea and even musculoskeletal complaints are recognised as health risks.[7]

---

[6]   See s789FD of the *Fair Work Act 2009* (Cth).
[7]   See p.14 of the Fair Work Commission's Anti-Bullying Benchbook.

The inclusion of mental health problems is vital as bullying at its most insidious is not physical: rather, it drives you to take up the bully's sabotage of your psyche. The bully can teach their victims to loathe themselves and to doubt their self-worth, making them hollow and psychologically destitute. At their worst, the bully can lead their victims to suicide—all without lifting a finger. It's a coward's way to commit violence against others; sadly, it is also devastatingly effective.

In my case, my boss's behaviour obviously fell within the definition of bullying. Her behaviour was protracted, unfair, and it made me feel abysmal. The case was clear, I felt, so in the week after I resigned I broke my silence and filed complaints with all the authorities. But all I got was bureaucratic evasion and an excoriating meeting with some spectre from HR.[8] There was sound and fury, but it signified everything except the chance things would change. And so today, my boss retains her position at the place I worked. My letters to her superiors, HR and the governmental bodies responsible for reprimanding people like her remain unanswered.

Though the organisation ignored my complaints, they still took the time to give me a parting present on my final day. My boss—the bully—gave me a gift card for an electronics store.[9] She also gave me a card where she wrote something like, 'All the best for your future.' I can't remember. A nice gift; but I would have preferred a voucher for therapy, especially since my future now involved going to therapy because of her. But who am I to judge? I wasn't expecting anything at all. And expecting nothing – that's the meaning of hopelessness, no?

---

[8] I.e., the department responsible for the proliferation of aforementioned R U OK? Day posters.

[9] Months later, I used the gift card to buy the hard drive where I store my writing. Because that's what I do now: I write so I can feel the texture of lives unknown. I write to capture and relieve the suffering of the world with words.

III
Narcissus & Echo

During the therapy sessions I've attended since I quit my job, I've discovered a strange feeling of gratitude towards my boss. This is not a case of Stockholm Syndrome, nor am I being ironic: I know her behaviour was appalling. My gratitude is sincere, for it was through her that I've learned more about care and human connection—about empathy.

With my analyst's help, I've developed an understanding of my boss's behaviour; in other words, I've learned about Narcissistic Personality Disorder & Its Discontents—me being a Discontent. I'm not a psychologist, but I believe my former boss behaved in a way that matched the diagnostic criteria for NPD.

The fifth edition of the psychiatrists' *Diagnostic & Statistical Manual*, or DSM-V, lists nine traits that characterise those with NPD. These people will generally have a grandiose sense of self-importance and are preoccupied with fantasies of unlimited success and power; they believe they are special, unique and that they deserve excessive admiration and the attention of high-status people or institutions; they are entitled, envious, arrogant and interpersonally exploitative; and, most importantly, they lack empathy and are unwilling to recognise or identify with the feelings and needs of others.

Although it is a painful and antisocial orientation to the world, NPD is surprisingly common. The DSM-V tells us that up to 6.2% of the adult population can be diagnosed with NPD.[10] But the real prevalence of narcissism may be greater still: the DSM-V requires the presence of at least five of these traits to substantiate a diagnosis of NPD, so people can exhibit damaging, narcissistic behaviours while they fall short of the diagnostic criteria. Given its prevalence, it's likely that many of us have been

---

[10] See *The Diagnostic & Statistical Manual of Mental Disorders: 5th Edition*, p.671.

hurt by narcissistic behaviour at some point, or have experienced
a relationship, be it professional, romantic or familial, with a
narcissistic person.
    I can't speak for my boss's inner world, yet her observable
behaviour fits comfortably into this diagnostic category. To her
employees, her sense of entitlement was painfully clear. She
expected others to comply with her protean, anarchic plans. We
had to immediately understand directions given in her
idiosyncratic, rambling and disjointed jargon, and it was our fault
if we failed to comprehend her.[11] A person who had dedicated
her adult life to ascending institutional hierarchies, it was also
clear that she was possessed by grandiose fantasies of success. In
meetings, she said we were to be 'the best,' yet she had no
discernible strategy for achieving this, nor did she ever define
what she meant by it. She had ambitions, but no plans; she had
visions, but was blind and, dominated by her dreams, she saw
little of the world. Her relationships with others were also a site
of suffering. Where she could choose kindness, she selected

---

[11] She had a first-rate talent for obfuscation: whenever a
    disagreement arose in a meeting, she would turn to her
    whiteboard, pen in hand, and would translate the argument into
    a series of mathematical operators, unconventional diagrams and
    strange tables, while, rhetorically, she would start to appeal to
    'pure logic' and the 'dictates of reason.' It would seem as though
    she was trying to help everyone understand; yet, as her rational
    soliloquy proceeded inexorably towards its only destination—
    that she, uniquely and in every instance, was correct—a strange
    transformation would occur. Language that first appeared
    reasonable was transmuted, subtly, almost alchemically, into its
    opposite: sense became nonsense. A horror at how imperceptible
    this process was. Eventually, she would finish writing and an
    acute sense of dread would envelope me: lost in the thick of
    symbols, I couldn't agree with her arguments—yet I had also lost
    my capacity to disagree. Her way of thinking made absolute
    within the room, placed beyond critique by language that was
    not unimpeachable but incomprehensible, we would all fall into
    silence, speechless and uneasy.

cruelty. She preferred indifference or malice when compassion was possible. Somehow, she wouldn't—or perhaps, couldn't—fully recognise or respect the subjectivity and dignity of others around her; her ability to empathise always fell short.

My boss did not see that we were emotionally vulnerable human beings. When I realise this, I began to wonder how she saw herself, or whether she could see herself at all. Given her treatment of me and others, it was as if the very ground of human relationships was barren in her, razed and salted; recognising this, I started to speculate. *Perhaps*, I thought, *she was not always this way. Maybe she has closed herself to other minds because she was also the victim of a great indignity.*

There is a clear, consistent structure to narcissistic behaviours, so it should be no surprise that the victims of narcissistic abuse are affected in a similar manner by the violence they experience. Those who suffer narcissistic abuse share a set of symptoms: they tend to become depressed, anxious and non-communicative; they dissociate from themselves, their surroundings and their emotions; they can feel impotent and passive, and unable to engage forthrightly with the external world; and their memories become obscure and diffuse, as though hidden behind a fog. Harmed by the narcissistic person's self-centred violence, the victim disappears spiritually. They are made hollow at the hands of their narcissistic master, who believes that subjectivity and autonomy are exceptional attributes to which only they are entitled. Through abuse the victim becomes a ghost; violence leaves them with a spectre's half-life.

Recently there has been increasing recognition of these victims' specific sufferings, and researchers have proposed a diagnostic category that reflects their findings. This new category is called 'Narcissistic Victim Syndrome,' and it groups together a constellation of symptoms that typify the suffering of those abused by narcissistic people. This is an important step towards helping those who have been harmed. Yet ironically, this syndrome's name contains a microcosmic repetition of the problem we encounter in narcissistic relationships: even while they try to heal, the person is defined as the narcissist's victim.

The name they give to their suffering, to their battered mind, retains the signature of their abuser; in a way, they remain shackled to their old master, and the ghost of violence haunts the victim even after they escape. Once again, the narcissistic person comes first.

For this reason, I prefer the more literary name for this form of pain: echoism.[12] 'Echoism' derives from the often-overlooked secondary character in the Greek Narcissus myth: Echo. In the tale's first part, Echo angers the gods, who inflict an elaborate punishment upon her: they strip her of her voice and her ability to express herself, condemning her to mimic the speech of others forevermore. They reduce Echo to an acoustic reflection, and in this state she falls in love with the irresistible Narcissus, a boy who is terrified of love and intimacy. She pursues Narcissus, echoing his words. Then, in a moment of fear—'I will die first, before thou shalt have the enjoyment of me,' Narcissus cries at her in Ovid's retelling—the beautiful youth violently rebukes her. In plangent despair, her body fades into nothingness, leaving only her voice, endlessly repeating his words. Echo loses her physical being, but her spirit remains enamoured with Narcissus: her voice forever bound to him, she watches on hopelessly as his self-absorption slowly kills him.

At the heart of this story lives a linguistic inequality. Despite his lack of care for others, Narcissus has the exceptional right to speak his mind while Echo is deprived of the ability to creatively use language. She is trapped in her mind, unable to communicate her own experiences to others, and forced to say only what she hears first. From our contemporary perspective, this is a particularly cruel and dehumanising fate for poor Echo. As we learn from Noam Chomsky's *Cartesian Linguistics*, philosophers across the Enlightenment period saw our linguistic creativity as fundamental to being human. For René Descartes and those who followed him, it was an essential mark of our humanity, being the decisive factor that separated us from animals. In an

---

[12]   I was introduced to the term in Donna Christina Savery's 2017 book, *Echoism: The Silenced Response to Narcissism*.

important sense, this is absolutely true. Unlike other species, we can all speak an unbounded number of unique, context-appropriate sentences. Amazingly, all humans are fundamentally creative, a point that Chomsky has emphasised for decades. Seeing Echo's fate in this light, we see that she was stripped of her humanity[13] when she was reduced to an eternal mimic. The gods denied Echo her creativity and made her into a reflection of those around her who remained entitled to autonomy. They eliminated her subjectivity: a cruel, terrible fate for human creatures.[14]

A subject of great violence, the Echo of Greek mythology is a repetition of another who speaks more powerfully than she, who, by an act of the gods, is forced to resonate and thrum with his words. The echoists of today share her fate. They are the people whose subjectivity is denied by the narcissistic people in their lives; whose creativity is thwarted by another's presence; and whose autonomy is overwritten by the violence of another's mind.

---

[13] Though Echo is a nature deity, she arguably has humanity in the Enlightenment-era ideological sense of the term that we are, admittedly, rather anachronistically projecting back onto this ancient Greek myth, i.e., she is capable of creative speech.

[14] Or at least, they deprived her of the ability to communicate her creative uses of language and express her subjectivity; we don't know what she experiences within. The myth, at least in Ovid's version, tells us nothing about how Echo feels about her entrapment in the language of others. Unable to express herself, to show the world her invisible heart by speaking, her despair was probably incomparable. I imagine that she suffered more than Narcissus himself, that accidious boy with his suicidal passivity, but unfortunately, we can't say for sure; all we have is our empathy to guide us. This leads us to an underemphasised aspect of the Narcissus myth: Echo's subjective and emotional experiences of her condition. I'm unsure whether this neglect is ironic, tragic or both; whatever the case, this decision echoes Narcissus' neglect of her emotions, and inscribes the story's content on its form.

By depriving their victims of their most essential humanity and their spontaneous creativity, the narcissistic person causes them great emotional suffering. But beyond this violence, we can detect another, greater tragedy that flows from narcissistic abuse: though they are the subject of abuse, the echoist may not be entirely innocent. Compelled to reflect the narcissistic person's image, the echoist changes over time, and can eventually become an abuser themselves. At least two things secure the echoist's transformation into a narcissistic abuser. Being bound to repeat the narcissistic person's words, the echoist reinforces the regime that dominates them; at the same time, they learn the language of their oppressor and can come to speak it themselves. Beyond this, they might dissociate from their emotions to survive their intolerable situation and while this can protect them from harm, it comes at a price: a lack of empathy. Our feelings are the source of our emotional knowledge of others. When we descend into numb solipsism, then, our empathy and introspection become impossible, leaving us ignorant of our own and others' emotions. Without our empathy, we lose what forestalls our own cruelty, priming us to inflict the same uncaring emotional violence on others that has so hurt us. Amid the violence, we may find ourselves remade in our abuser's image: from Echo another Narcissus is born.[15]

Another's cruelty can encourage us to be cruel to ourselves and others; the greatest horror of narcissistic violence and the echoistic defence, then, is its self-perpetuating nature. Psychologists know that echoism has a tragic nature, as victims of narcissistic abuse regularly mimic the actions of their oppressors. In this light, the narcissistic person must become a more sympathetic character to us. An abuser's inability to accept our humanity may have been a rational response to their environment at some point. Maybe they, like their present victims, were once the Echo of another petty Narcissus; maybe

---

[15] I owe a debt to Daniel Shaw's *Traumatic Narcissism: Relational Systems of Subjugation* for these thoughts about narcissistic abuse.

they now live at the nadir of tragedy, animated today by the ghosts of violence past and forever trapped in the language of their own abuser. In the centre of every Echo there lies Narcissus' eternal sighs; our empathy demands that we recognise this and accept that the biggest victim may be the abuser herself.

IV
A Leader's Trauma

We deplore the narcissistic person's violence today; yet we now see they may be a tragic figure. Once a victim themselves, the defences they erected to survive can draw them into cruelty and violence. The narcissistic victim may reach for power over others to combat their powerlessness, and so inflict impotence on those they choose to dominate. They may become an abuser themselves.

This is a terrible fate. Yet the irony does not end with their transformation from victim to abuser. Deepening the tragic disposition their oppressor inscribed upon them, the narcissistic victim's bid for power can worsen their trauma and narcissism, because authority itself is a traumatic experience. The narcissistic defence that pushes the victim towards power can be exacerbated by the emotional damage power entails, so the victim can become more narcissistic as they ascend whatever hierarchy they give themselves to. As such, we cannot simply devote our empathy to the echoist, or the narcissistic person as a victim. We must also adopt a 'radical empathy'[16] towards them as an authority or leader too. Naturally, we are not inclined to

---

[16]   The *New York Times'* Ben Ratliff described Anohni's work as an example of 'radical' empathy. To me, radical empathy seems to mean nothing more than 'really strong and deliberate empathy with people you don't usually care about'. It also tells us basically everything we need to know about our society that empathy is conceived as a radical political act.

give empathy to authorities that dominate others. But as an examination of pop-singer Anohni's art reveals, such radical empathy is indispensable if we are to resolve the problem of narcissism.

In 2016,[17] I learned of so-called 'radical empathy' through Anohni's nauseatingly beautiful single, 'Drone Bomb Me,' the opening track from her record *Hopelessness*. Sung from the 'perspective of a girl seeking death after her family was killed in

---

[17] Anohni was only one of three artists that shifted my view of empathy that year. First, I encountered Brian Eno explaining that the critical function of art is to make us imagine new worlds, which he said 'helps us experience empathy.' Then, in *Although of Course You End Up Becoming Yourself,* I read David Foster Wallace explaining that good writing is premised upon empathy. For him, 'the writer should remind the reader of how smart the reader is... I just think to look across the room and automatically assume that somebody else is less aware than me, or that somehow their interior life is less rich, and complicated, and acutely perceived than mine, makes me not as good a writer. Because that means I'm going to be performing for a faceless audience, instead of trying to have a conversation with a person... I've started to think it's my biggest asset as a writer. Is that I'm pretty much just like everybody else.' Both Eno and Wallace make excellent points, but I think we can be more radical. Art doesn't merely rely on empathy or help us experience it. The imaginative experience and production of art, for both creator and observer, literally *is* empathy, because art both relies on and produces emotional knowledge of the self and others. The creation and release of art are communicative/perceptive acts that deepen our knowledge of human life, and the subjective experience of the self and others. And so, the experience of art, especially if it is good, produces precisely the same kind of knowledge and psychological experience in the creator and their audience as empathy. Art, then, is always a form of empathy, while the experience of art provokes empathy.

a drone attack,'[18] this track finds Anohni in the emotional warscape of a child orphaned by brutally indifferent and uncaring US foreign policy. Torn from her loved ones, the young girl seeks the same death as her mother and father. She hopes for death by drone strike, to be killed by a machine operated by somebody hundreds or thousands of miles away to whom she is nothing more than a monochrome blur, a slur of pixels on a digital screen. 'Drone bomb me,' Anohni sings over a shattering, glassy beat. 'Blow my head off / Explode my crystal guts.'

Anohni's desires here are devastating; adopting this perspective and relaying its violent fantasies are shocking moves for a pop singer. Yet her artistic act goes beyond simple provocation. By taking this girl's terrible and terribly real perspective, her horror-fantasies of exploding 'crystal guts', Anohni forces us to understand the plights of those subject to US imperialism around the globe, making the track a withering criticism of Barack Obama's presidential administration. Under Obama's authority, 26,171 bombs were dropped on foreign countries in 2016 alone.[19] Some of these were fired from drones in the kind of attacks that killed at least 300 civilians during his presidency.[20] These are atrocious acts, and by way of Anohni's surprising empathy for this imagined young girl, we see Obama's violence in all its stratospheric height. Anohni makes us feel dwarfed by his savagery, and so reveals the vast human suffering he inflicted during his presidency.

I am staggered by Anohni's artistic act on this record. Whenever I listen to it, my nerve endings feel electric, exposed, properly scintillated. It makes me yearn for abstract things—

---

[18] The quote is from *Pitchfork's* review of the single. See https://pitchfork.com/reviews/tracks/18084-anohni-drone-bomb-me/

[19] See https://www.theguardian.com/commentisfree/2017/jan/09/america-dropped-26171-bombs-2016-obama-legacy

[20] See https://www.nytimes.com/2019/03/30/opinion/drones-civilian-casulaties-trump-obama.html

beauty, the sublime, etc. Hearing it, I want to unfold and weep. For in a hopelessly inadequate but nonetheless substantial way— for how could we really understand this girl's world, whatever our efforts?—Anohni leads us to understand the emotions of victims we neglect or ignore. [21] An extraordinary empathy is Anohni's brave artistic achievement on this record; with her, we see how empathy can produce knowledge of the world's atrocities.

Anohni's work also shows how merely witnessing an act of radical understanding, even when we are neither the subject nor object of compassion, can make us cry for change. The sight of another's empathy can crack open our entombed hearts. And in the moment of breach, when emotion floods into our blood, where the spray of feeling hits our mind, we can see a new future. Anohni shows us that all our own desperation for a world less impoverished of connection, less lonely, and more compassionate, is brought into the light when we reach for another. When Anohni calls for mutual understanding, we find a reflection of ourselves; through her, we see our depths, our shallows, all the things that we lack. We also see that our image is an image of the other—even those others subject to violence we could prevent—and we realise that the indignity of our situation is undeniable. All this, we learn from Anohni on one song: it's the fruit of what we call 'radical empathy.'

---

[21] Anohni's artistic success on this track is related to our ultimate failure to fully understand the girl's emotions. Her suffering is so profound that our attempt to understand it gives us some knowledge of her experience, while also highlighting how inadequate our imaginations are when counterpoised against the reality of her world. The success of empathy as an epistemic experience is, in a way, related to our failure to fully comprehend the other's alterity; we only know the other by recognising that we do not fully know them. A complete empathy is always related to both our understanding and the failure thereof— to insufficiency, in a word.

Anohni's record is a search for knowledge of the suffering that lives in forgotten hearts; it unveils the darkest corners of ourselves. When I listen to the album, I wonder how Obama would respond to *Hopelessness*, a work whose title deliberately inverts his 2008 campaign slogan, 'Hope.' The record is drenched in despair, and its sadness is mostly justified: during his tenure Obama slumped from hope to hopelessness with every move. After his election he quickly became a figure of cruel irony: he began his presidency by bailing out Wall Street in 2009 and he closed it by bombing a Syrian children's hospital in 2016. [22] Obama regularly fell short of his own rhetoric and ethical standards; by campaigning on such an optimistic platform, he set the stage for his own tragic decline.

As Obama moved from failure to failure, hollowing out whatever was left of his optimistic vision, Anohni became a negative dialectician. On her album, she adopts a militant, critical attitude to uncover the bleak undertone of his lucent words. For his weak action on climate change, we get '4 Degrees,' a doomy cut that speaks of 'tiny creatures,' burning. For Obama's failure to abolish the death penalty, we get 'Execution,' which includes the crushingly judgemental lyrics: 'Execution/It's an American Dream.' In pop music, it's rare to see a political lyric that captures the ferocious sadness that comes with the progressive commitment to justice. Still more uncommon are statements so unhappily justified by the acts of our leaders.

As listeners, we are struck by the weight of Anohni's lyrics. The burden of truth gives them heft and impact. Nonetheless, I believe she falls short politically. Though she takes great pains to tear off the shackles of indifference and look her leader's brutality in the face, and while she imagines the perspectives of those most marginalised by his regime, she fails to extend her empathy to one, final character: Obama himself.

Anohni ignores the suffering of the leader who made these terrible decisions. Yet this last act is essential for I believe Obama was neither callous nor evil; rather, he was compromised. In

---

[22]   See https://www.bbc.com/news/world-middle-east-37998751

2015, Obama admitted his failures to Yanis Varoufakis in a conversation about the GFC. 'You must know that I was forced to do things that were very hard for me,' he said, 'things that I did not want to do. Things that amounted to political poison… I had to collaborate with people that had created the problem.'[23] In a moment of apparent self-awareness, Obama candidly admits his shortcomings and asks for Varoufakis' empathy. His words may be hollow and self-serving—we must note Obama was then the world's most powerful man who had the ability, duty and choice to avoid atrocities—yet we can also hear them with sympathy. While Obama was never wholly deprived of his autonomy, the constraints his power and political circumstance imposed upon his liberty must have been immense. Extending our empathy to Obama, I believe we can hear the pain in his words, the sadness of a man pressed to choose cruelty while preaching its opposite—even if Anohni chooses not to do so.

I doubt Obama wanted to become a hypocrite. But irrespective of his hopes and intentions, he became one; acknowledging this, we glimpse the trauma inherent to leadership. Our leaders are not victims of any person's abuse, but they suffer greatly under the demands of authority. We cannot deny that Obama committed atrocities and that he should be ashamed of his actions; we should bring him to justice. Yet we can also see that leadership is a traumatic experience. Circumstances command our leaders to resolve the disjunctions between desire and action by smothering their hearts. Leadership's traumas push people towards numbness and solipsism; like emotional abuse, its tensions can encourage leaders to become narcissistic. The pains of authority can force us to stop our introspection and withhold our empathy from others as a means of self-protection. And there lies the rub. If a lack of empathy underlies atrocities, it is unsurprising that our leaders so frequently fail their responsibilities to others: their position atop a hierarchy of power directly encourages it.

---

[23] *Adults in the Room*, p.375.

Leadership encourages an ethic of self-repression that can lead to narcissistic withdrawal; perhaps this ethic, seen so clearly in Obama, is part of the reason a leader's empathy vanishes. It seems that leadership itself undermines empathy; tragically, it eliminates the social abilities that originally make us desirable leaders. [24]

During his presidency, Obama did not ask for hopelessness. Yet like Anohni, like the little girl who lost her parents to a drone strike, he became a victim of a system antithetical to empathy. We should not explain his behaviour only by referring to this system's effects, for this would amount to a rejection of human autonomy; yet we also should not make Obama solely responsible for his atrocities. The system and the individual must be tried. While Anohni's acts of radical empathy remain vital and essential, then, they don't go far enough. With Anohni, we see that it takes an enormous effort to understand a victim's humanity when it has been denied. But her omission suggests it is harder still to comprehend the humanity of the violent perpetrator. To do so, we must understand how inhumanity

---

[24] Our literary sensibilities immediately take to this claim, yet recent neuroscientific research illuminates this tragic connection between leadership, power and empathy. In an article for *The Atlantic* called 'Power Causes Brain Damage,' we learn that empathy deficits are common for those in positions of power; power, it seems, also exacerbates them. Personal empowerment leads to neurological changes in people akin to brain damage. In power, we become 'more impulsive, less risk-aware, and, crucially, less adept at seeing things from other people's point of view.' Power also anaesthetises a neural process called 'mirroring' that scientists think is responsible for empathy. This leads them to 'stop simulating the experience of others,' creating an empathy deficit that can't be deliberately reversed by the subject. Powerful people have neither the time nor cognitive capacity to consider the nuanced subjectivity of every person who works for them. This would be impossible, so dampening our empathy is a somewhat adaptive response to power.

takes root at the centre of another person's soul. How living, breathing others can commit atrocities, and nonetheless remain human beings capable of ethics and reflection. This is incredibly difficult, but only if we do this can we complete the most challenging task of all: the cultivation of an accurate picture of humanity that accepts all these contradictions together. To do 'radical empathy', we must empathise with the victim, whose humanity is denied, and the oppressor, who denies their own humanity, and conclude that the chance to be humane, inhumane or both at once is a basic condition and a perennial possibility of our lives, and that our place in hierarchies of power can affect our predisposition to cruelty and violence.

Until we try to understand those who commit atrocities or abuse, the process of empathy is incomplete. We will remain purblind until we ask our leaders what traumas and sufferings were symbiotic with their actions. But this is never an apologist's exercise in pardoning atrocities. It is merely a recognition that, without scrupulous accounting that contains all available information, justice cannot be done. We want bespoke solutions, as justice that is not made to fit will always hold spaces where injustice can grow. To avoid injustice, we must see and understand the emotional experience of everyone, be they victims or abusers; we must practise a complete, radical empathy that extends to everyone involved in the situation wherever we hope to do politics.

V
R UR CORPORATIONS OK?

By comparing Obama and Anohni, we see power itself may be irretrievably flawed. If so, this has implications for corporate mental health days, which, following the gargantuan efforts of mental health activists, medical professionals, political and corporate leaders and HR departments everywhere, have become a global phenomenon.

Since 2009, Australians have observed R U OK? Day on the second Thursday of September. Currently, the day is something of a national institution. Organisations all over the country put up posters, send out emails, and have nice little talks with snacks. The R U OK? Day brand, with its mad yellow and black logo, incorporating a smiley face inexplicably scrubbed of its eyes—an interesting choice given that the day is all about empathy, i.e., it asks us to see the subjectivity of others—has become ubiquitous. Here, workers are all aware that we need to be aware of mental health problems; Australia heralds the metacognitive revolution.

For at least a moment every year, our corporations try to foster a compassionate atmosphere among their employees. They take a moment to recognise the real, beating human hearts that throb beneath the thin veneer of our corporate personalities. Though there is an obvious profit motive underlying the corporate recognition of mental health issues, the meaning of the day transcends banal cynicism. For some, this can be a moment of genuine relief. The façade we adopt at work is stifling after a while, and frequently, it's built up in moments of defensiveness: at times where we—in fear of losing our livelihoods or committing some cosmic solecism that would condemn us to the dead-ends of obscure corporate offices, our flesh sagging into synthetic leather under halogen lights, or worse, to the abyss of unemployment—choose to hide whatever comes spontaneously to us.

R U OK? Day is a moment of freedom. At its glimmering best, we see co-workers confess their struggles, and recognising ourselves in their words, we feel our humanity expand. We might learn that the odd guy from the statistics department with outlandish opinions and obsessive hobbies, or the pugnacious septuagenarian who should've retired years ago and whom people are worried might keel over and just die at his desk, or the oleaginous, ascendant maverick whose life seems suspiciously frictionless, or that tragically obsequious intern who looks exceptionally prim but is nonetheless paronychiatic, chewing her nails down to the hyponychium all the time, feel the same way we do about the world. To learn of the despair and anxieties of others, and that, even in the invisible part of others, their elusive minds, we can find something like ourselves is very reassuring; these moments of discovery, of empathy, make us all feel less twisted and weird and deeply estranged from the people around us who, contrary to their fleshy, lugubrious appearances, could be phantoms, automatons, or an entirely different form of life to us with a totally alien inner life. Through communication, we find community; and by empathising with our co-workers' specific struggles we can find something universal, or at least something shared and communal, about being human.

The compassionate conversation of R U OK? Day can be a tremendous good. It reduces our sense of alienation while raising awareness about terribly common psychological ailments. But even more importantly, it helps us create a culture of empathy, a public good whose benefits are relational, communal and essential. For when we ask R U OK? the compassionate listener discovers something about the other and about themselves. By answering it, the courageous speaker gains the chance to complete the image of themselves in the listener's mind, and they can see how they are received. Each party catches a glimpse of themselves through the other's eyes, leading to an improved knowledge of the self, others and relationships for all involved. By trying to know the other through communication, we come to know ourselves; and by knowing ourselves, we also come to know them. Through empathic conversation we learn more about what it is to be human, and we leave with a greater ability to work communally, to relate to others, and to love. We also liberate ourselves from emotions that may otherwise fester and decay and mutate in the dark, growing from possibly minor, transient impressions to pervasive anxieties and depressions. So, when we ask and respond to the question, R U OK?, we gain something vital. With language and communication, we reveal ourselves and our common humanity and we find salvation from the atrocities propagated by emotional silence.

Collective mental health depends on empathic communication. R U OK? Day tries to promote and revivify our faith in communication because we all have a responsibility to ourselves and others to live, speak, listen and think well. So, when a corporation asks its workers if they R OK, should we expect it to improve its self-understanding?[25] Can we rely on our leaders, whose role involves traumas and stressors, and who are more likely to be drawn from empathic communication and into narcissistic self-enclosure due to their responsibilities, to step outside their lonely place at the peak of the hierarchy and really speak, and to hear in return? One would hope so. Yet in my experience, my organisation's promotion of R U OK? Day felt like a deeply ironic joke; a symbol of hopelessness. Despite her legal, moral and social responsibilities to behave otherwise, my former boss used her powers to terrorise her subordinates. With her abusive words, she transformed communication from salvation into brutality. She shattered the possibility of collective understanding and care at her workplace; by observing R U OK? Day while behaving this way, she emptied the day of its meaning.

This contradictory experience is a disappointing outcome for R U OK? Day. Yet I wonder if it isn't unique to my previous workplace. In fact, I suspect my ordeal might be a simple exaggeration of the norm—an archetype of the everyday experience. As we learned from Obama, a peril of leadership is that empowerment inhibits our empathy. Where some hold power over others, everybody is pressed to diminish their empathy, which, tragically, is the psychological barrier that prevents the abusive behaviour that harms our ability to empathise with one another. Accordingly, so long as we have hierarchies and power differentials at work, we'll find leaders whose empathy is diminished by their responsibilities and subordinates who suffer their abuses. If this is correct, then there is an issue with the structure of workplaces in general. If power promotes a decline in empathy, and this increases the likelihood of abusive, narcissistic behaviours among leaders, which causes withdrawn, echoistic behaviour in employees, then a culture of bullying is the logical consequence of our structures of authority.

---

[25] Keeping in mind that today corporations have a personality at law.

An empathy-deficient ecosystem is a predictable outcome of leadership itself. If we scrutinise the structure of the workplace, we find the pattern of traumatic authority repeated *ad nauseum*. Noam Chomsky often refers to corporations as 'private tyrannies.'[26] He is right, of course, for when we sign the dotted line and give our leaders a virtually absolute, final say on our actions, we willingly agree to a form of dictatorship. The labour contract is an embodiment of pure, undemocratic authority, and it's fundamental to our institutions under contemporary capitalism that leaders and subordinates are unequal in knowledge, influence and authority. Such inequalities persist at the heart of most corporations, and so our enterprises are premised on relationships that compromise our ability to understand one another while we work together. Economists like Joseph Stiglitz often say we work today in a 'knowledge economy.' Ironically, its workplaces are epistemic dead zones that stifle human understanding by inhibiting our empathy for others.

Things need not be this way. Though they are rare, it's possible to create democratic workplaces where conversations are free and reciprocal, and where leaders counteract the forces that encourage their narcissism through empathic listening. If we desired, we could give everybody in our workplaces an equal voice that is both influential and respected. We could let workers autonomously or collectively decide on the direction of their work. And we could create an environment where people do not feel the need to hide and repress themselves. In short, we could democratise our workplaces; we could give ourselves dignity; and yet we choose not to do so. Collectively, we tend to prefer workplaces where we can be dismissed for contradicting our leaders, where we must smother our dissenting impulses to preserve our income, where we allow ourselves and others to suffer in silence for fear of reprimand, delivered by an authority who might abuse us and over whom we hold little influence. For whatever reason, we prefer relationships of command; tyranny

---

[26] *Consequences of Capitalism*, p.86.

and inequality predominate where reciprocity, care and empathy could prevail. It is clear, then: our leaders and corporations are NOT OK. And for as long as we work within such structures, neither are we.

VI
The Solution

When I resigned from my role at the business, a conflagration burned in my heart. The failure of empathy is traumatic, and I burned with violent anger and acid resentment towards my boss. Even today, while my memory of the organisation is hopelessly opaque, the pain is unforgettable.

I must respond to my pain. Fearing a repetition of these events, I could slam the doors of my psyche shut and repress this trauma for the sake of silence. Perhaps this would work for a while. But in the long run, it would do me the worst harm of all possible solutions: it could turn me into someone like her, giving me a tragic destiny, where I repeat the failures that caused me so much pain and do to others what I could not tolerate myself.

I don't want this. So, in the wake of agony, I cannot deny myself knowledge of what happened. I can't obscure the pain. Doing so will leave me ignorant, blind and unable to avoid repetition. So now, I'll speak: instead of hatred, rather than fury, I feel sorrow. In truth, my heart breaks when I think that my boss didn't have it within herself to treat me or anybody else with empathy and care. The rapacious loneliness of her violent disposition, the boundless fear of others it entails—this, *this* must be truly intolerable. Hers is an impossible burden, and I hope she finds relief someday—for both her present pain, and for whatever abuses in her past may have led her to become an abuser herself.

From my empathy for my boss, I turn towards a desire for justice. Here, our empathy grounds a responsibility[27] that she failed. For if we are to empathise truly with another, we must not stop at the point where we gain an understanding of their suffering. Once their pain has been exposed to the light, we must also demand their responsibility. For while our empathy locates the roots of their barbarism in their private anguish, it also reveals the human capacity for freedom, introspection, healing and self-overcoming. We find liberty, rationality, compassion and the capacity for transformation in ourselves through introspection: if we do not want to repeat their narcissistic cruelty and selfish exceptionalism, we must ascribe these traits we find within ourselves to them. The narcissistic abuser is both wounded and capable of healing: while the abuser may be damaged, our empathy demands their empathy, and it necessitates that we hold them responsible. Through empathy, we can bring the abuser's narcissistic cruelties to consciousness; through empathy, we make their unconscious defences unethical and we can demand justice from those unwilling to cease their abuse of others. Empathy allows us to make a demand. To my boss, we say: *change, or, on the grounds of cruelty and incompetence, abdicate your position of power.*

We now turn to the corporation itself. Understanding the nature of power, we see that we must change the system that produces narcissistic abusers and their woeful Echoes. Asking R U OK? is a movement towards solving workplace abuse, a scourge responsible for much psychological suffering in our society. But it's not enough. While it is a bid for a communal, relational experience, it usually occurs in an environment bereft of real community and relationships, where inequality prevails, where people are defined by differences in their power and

---

[27] The notion of responsibility is also connected to the notions of empathic listening and speech; etymologically, the word responsibility comes from the Latin *respondere*, meaning 'respond, answer to, promise in return.'

where communication is constrained. We ask the question in an environment that inexorably tends towards abuse.

Unless we remove the barriers to empathy between leaders and their followers, our empathic gestures will always be limited in their effectiveness. So when we ask R U OK? the question must extend to our friends, colleagues and subordinates. At the same time, it must reach upwards to the organisation and its leaders, who must then recognise the voices of their workers and change their behaviours. A free and democratic clamour of honest expression must prevail; silence cannot reign over issues of abuse. We must also extend our questioning to the nature of authority itself and ask: IS THE SYSTEM OK? Currently, our working arrangements are premised upon an inequality that encourages narcissistic abuse. It isn't clear that the authority endemic to the labour contract is compatible with empathy.

Until this political issue that defangs empathy is resolved, our society will always have room for unnecessary inhumanity. We need a properly emotional dialogue between all levels of our organisations and all levels of our own psyches. We need the right to speak and listen openly both within ourselves and with others. We need this in every area of our lives and our societies. And so, we need democracy in the workplace. For without democracy, a form of governance that is inextricable from the right to listen and speak freely and from positions of equal power, our organisations, relationships and subjectivities will remain divided, spinning between yellow and vengeful, sun-like burning and the quiet and black depths of despair, split by the unjust inequality of our world. Such an outcome is intolerable; it is tragic. Yet unless we repair the fissure that lies at the heart of our society, the rend in empathy, this kind of contradiction and suffering will prevail and events like R U OK? Day will be forever mired in contradiction.

Love & Meaning
(a.k.a. *Metroid: Fusion v Molloy*)

'A madman is not someone who has lost his reason but someone who has lost everything but his reason'
—G. K. Chesterton

I
Free Association

AT AGE 17 I STOPPED PLAYING VIDEO GAMES and I became anxious about the meaning of life. I turned away from the screen, and I realised existence was finite. I put down the controller, and I knew death was inevitable—a 'blood-black nothingness'[1] that came for us all. I traded Japanese games for French novels; I became existential and time—the idea of time, the passage thereof—became important. *Oui, je suis très existentiel.* I joined the cult of value, the religion of purpose. The work, whatever it was, needed to start. To be productive, efficient. This was paramount. Time and waste, the economic principle. Games had no place in the world of meaning, so I exiled them from my life. Forgot them. Amnesia was necessary for living. Something like a rite of passage. No time for games anymore. Begin your life in the grip of significance.

At age 21 I dated a woman who asked if I played games. Could see in her eyes that she was preparing to discriminate, discard me as a partner. I understood this. I accepted this. God no, I told her. Total waste of time. I use my time for valuable things. Self-improvement: reading, studying, running, writing, working, doing. I mostly try to improve the self. Too busy for games. The self must be improved. Her expectant face slackened a little. Oh good, she said. My ex played all the time. I hated it. *Great*, I

---

[1] *Pale Fire*, p.50.

thought. *I'm militantly against whatever he did. I'll disavow all the past you won't like. Forget whatever I was.* She later told me she had a five-item checklist for prospective dating partners. Evidently I passed. How powerful, the need to improve the self.

At age 23, a little peccadillo. I confess: I relapsed. I bought *The Legend of Zelda: Breath of the Wild.* I couldn't resist. *Ocarina of Time* was my first love, and *Breath of the Wild,* an open-world Zelda—to play it satisfied an impossible desire I dreamed as a child. Make of that what you will. And my second love? A girl who also loved *Ocarina.* Sat next to her in second grade, heart beaming radiospirals of wordless intensity. Later I learned this was called 'desire,' and then I learned to forget it. For what time do we have for love when we live in the grip of significance? Make of that what you will.

Today, at age 26, I am undergoing a course of psychoanalysis.[2] Twice a week. Soliloquies in a soundproofed room. Ornately carpeted with aureate trim. A photo of Freud with dogs hangs in the waiting room. Usually, the famous couch stands solemnly,

---

[2] WHY I CHOSE PSYCHOANALYSIS: The rational administration of emotional life is an ethic promoted by contemporary models of psychotherapy—cognitive behavioural therapy, acceptance and commitment therapy, etc. In my experience, these therapies teach patients to scrutinise themselves constantly, and to correct and control their behaviour through conscious action, making them homologous with rational ideology, which aims for the control of uncertainty through technical knowledge. Though they espouse mindfulness etc., in CBT, the patient is effectively taught to impose judgement upon their thought: a problematic and rather pathological suggestion, given that the negative affect that brought them to therapy is frequently produced by some hidden, latent judgement that has confined them since childhood. Psychoanalysis, however, posits that the identification of that original judgement can liberate the patient from the negative emotions—bypassing the need for conscious control, making CBT techniques redundant. Given this, I chose psychoanalysis for its transformative, rather than its administrative, potential.

just over my analyst's shoulder, but it is currently out for reupholstering. Overuse. A pile of cushions in its place, signifying absence. (Do we mourn the couch, the analysand's symbol of potential, of words and memories freed, but now of futures lost?) Across the room, books everywhere. Stacks of words pressed against words. Oblong columns of light askance on the covers. Reich, Klein, Goethe, Rilke, *Infinite Jest*, *Pale Fire*. The Nabokov I know about. Saw it in a photo on his website. Sent my email because of it. Felt I could trust him to understand. John Shade's 719th line: 'the strange world where I was a mere stray.'[3] When I first arrived I spied David Foster Wallace lurking in the cabinet. This confirmed my choice. I could trust him to understand. He would know what they mean. What I mean.

All my clothes now smell of sage. My analyst asked if he could burn it while we talk. I said he could. Olfactory stimulation, mnemonic prompting. Didn't know it would scent my wardrobe so. We often make jokes about fascism, authoritarianism. The isms are all fair game. We laugh about ideology, the irrational excesses of a rational culture. He burns the sage. The burning is probably important, and I don't mind it at all. Maybe it works.

We talk and later I dream. Then we talk some more. This has an effect: my abandoned fantasies, overgrown and wild, ragged around the edges—these, return in the night. Asleep, I see furtive glimpses of secrets. The lost, the banished, the forgotten; words once said and futures once seen, unearthed and recalled, summoned by the sage. Hopefully the air doesn't damage the evidence. Turn to dust under weight of light. I said I don't mind the burning, okay?

Awake, these dreams lead me to say insightful things. Like how I first experienced depression when I turned 17. Like how I got depressed when I needed to decide what to do with my life, also age 17. A wronged rite of passage; a bad relationship, then collapse into anhedonia. The words I say when I smell the sage. I tell my analyst I can see a pattern-like sadness I've repeated ever since, intensity rising every round. And as I speak I discover that

---

3   Ibid, p.51.

when my depression first came, it felt uncannily familiar to me. Like I knew it, even though I knew I didn't know it. But maybe I didn't know I knew it. I don't know. Just stop talking about the burning.

One night last week, I finished John Banville's novel, *The Sea*, a spirited tribute to the memory-dense Nabokovian novel that depicts a man possessed by the spectres of trauma. 'The past beats inside me like a second heart,' the protagonist writes, pressed by the presence of an absent world. Always the protagonist is remembering, recalling his ordeals, the deaths of his loves. He lives like a ghost in his own past, like he is 'there and not there, myself and revenant, immured in the moment and yet hovering somehow on the point of departure.'[4] *The Sea* was a good book; it made me confront the spectres of what I've lost and what remains, the ghosts of futures that never came. But as Banville's gold dust settled in my mind, a great swirl of psychic wind scattered its impressions. From the shadowland of my psyche, an encaged memory blasted forth. Starved and slightly feral, a purplish tinge to its skin given the lack of light. The return of the repressed. I put the book down, and my mind made me relive a childhood memory, an event that haunted and terrorised me, aged ten.

Images and sounds, dust-covered but clearly unforgotten, swirled through my mind. Don't laugh. But somehow I had unearthed a need to replay a certain video game. A childhood favourite. One my father bought me as a reward years ago. Who knows what triggers these things. Sage? I can't say. I only know my heart was set: I had to replay Nintendo's *Metroid: Fusion*.[5]

---

[4] *The Sea*, p.10 and p.98.

[5] *METROID: FUSION*: this is a 2004 Nintendo® GameBoy™ Advance game, starring Samus Aran, ferocious heroine[a] of previous instalments of the Metroid franchise. Alone on a space station infested with a deadly parasite, Samus must fight for her survival, stalked by a powerful clone of herself: the fearsome SA-X. The game is moderately difficult, and takes probably six hours

to complete, depending on how often you die, whether you're playing with a guide, the exact curvature of the inverse-U relationship between your technical competence and your level of frustration, anxiety, etc.

[a] Aran's femininity has been a weird, vaguely unsettling source of pride for the gaming industry since the first *Metroid* game was released in the late '80s. Much to the surprise of players, upon finishing the game the visibly sex/gender ambiguous avatar they had controlled, and had therefore assumed was male, i.e. like every other game they played, shed its armour, revealing a scantily clad and ostensibly lipsticked (admittedly, it's hard to say this for sure, given the low pixel count) woman. The designers ensured that her blatant and intentional nubility was undeniable, her being all hips, mammarially endowed, with luscious Pantene-ad red hair, and garbed in a deeply unpragmatic, lingerie-esque hot pink[i] bra and panty combo, instead of a more pragmatic, given the situation, sports bra, which existed in the real world in the 1980s (i.e. when the game was developed), the 'Free Swing Tennis Bra' having been introduced in 1975 by Glamorise Foundations, Inc., and a futuristic variant of which Samus almost certainly could have bought for herself in some high-tech, future shopping environment before her foray onto planet Zebes. According to at least one commentator cited on Wikipedia, this, i.e. the reveal of Samus' femininity, was the original 'jaw-dropping moment in gaming,' a claim that unfortunately says much more about the somewhat outmoded vision of gender held by gamers/game designers than the purported progressive credibility of the industry as a whole. That a person in a blocky and unrevealing military exoskeleton—at least as it was back then, as Samus' Varia suit now accentuates her vanishingly narrow waist—could be a woman was allegedly shocking to gamers, the revelation apparently being that women, just like their male counterparts, could also coldly and robotically perform acts of violence over and over without succumbing to exhaustion, or acknowledging the subjective trauma of such acts, or questioning to any significant extent the overall purpose of the mission or the authorities behind it, the latter of which, for a somewhat unfathomable reason, is a feature *Metroid* players actually like—that is, the sense of blind, directionless exploration, unprompted by in-game instructions. This last point seems to be a necessary element to the pre-Oedipal space of gaming described by Žižek elsewhere in this essay—i.e., its guilt-free vacuum

As we live, forever the return of emotional ghosts. Old feelings and languages resurface in time, stepping elegantly from the shadows, enticement and thought revived once again. This should not be a surprise. However ephemeral, every emotion and word once had a home in our head. Maybe that home fell into disrepair, becoming dilapidated and decrepit, a disgrace to its former glory. But only a tremendous violence can truly destroy the psychic structure and clear up the rubble without a trace. To lose a home, we must lose our memory, become an amnesiac. But few of us can deliberately pursue such feats of neural architecture or mnemonic demolition; both presence and absence signify the banished. To eliminate both and sweep the mind clean of being and un-being: to truly forget, nothing less than an erasure of absence is required. A difficult, impossible demand. Hence, we are haunted, and our most passionate spirits linger. The shopping mall built over a crushed home forever holds the ghosts of the family rushed off the land. They haunt us, they dance in the flickering of halogen lights, they live in reflections cracked and distorted on the marmoreal floors. Dig and you'll find them, these desires, memories and words. Exhume, unbury, remember; free them and be free. Speak, memory. Or don't if you can't cope. Whatever you can live with.

---

suffused with fantasy (esp. sexual, which explains Samus' underwear choice), the physical manifestation of a psychological world unruptured by paternal authority, i.e., one without direction.

[i] The exact colour is HTML/HEX code: #e7005b. It is a precisely flattering shade for her skin tone (#f0d0b0) that exactly matches her lipstick and boots, but which unfortunately clashes a little with her hair (#e75f13). In reality, she would probably look devastating in a #000000 shade (i.e., black) underwear ensemble, but this would render her sexualised areas indistinguishable from the background texture, eliminating what is probably, and disappointingly, the whole point of Samus' femininity.

II
Metroid: Fusion & *Molloy*

Drenched in memory, I downloaded *a Metroid* emulator, started a new game. Six days later, it was done: I had replayed the game, relived my memories.

During this week of *Metroid,* I expected to feel guilt whenever I loaded the game. Time and waste, the economic principle. But as I played, I barely thought for hours at a time. In *Metroid* I found focus, a rare moment where the flow of consciousness slowed. The freshet of ideas, the concept-inundation, diminished from deluge to trickle. An absence of thought created the space to remember how gaming can bring on a state of suspension; how it holds the chance for relief.

Meaning-anxiety was impossible for me while I played *Metroid.* Žižek wrote about this, the underlying psychoanalytic reason for gaming's appeal. Ideas trickling back. He said something like: enamoured with its mechanisms of punishments and rewards, confronted with frustrations we can always overcome, in games we 'float freely' relieved of 'guilt and death.'[6] With our unlimited lives and chances for repetition, we are divorced from death and time. Meaning leaves us, and we are unmoored from our bodies. Emotions are free to rush and retreat, and we become something pure and sublime, intensely immanent yet deeply transcendent. An unrestricted flux of desire.

Immersed in *Metroid,* digital spirits sprinted through my mind. As I entered every room and found it exactly as it was fifteen years before, a spectral nostalgia condensed behind my eyes. Whenever the SA-X—Samus' clone that acts as the game's antagonist—appeared on-screen, an ancient, primordial anxiety returned; I was consumed by a fear that echoed my child-terror from those lost days. All these old emotions resurfaced, unearthing the terrors and the images, inextricably bound, that had lain dormant in my bones for years.

---

[6]   *Sex & The Failed Absolute*, p.171.

The memories. All week, burning with revived desires, I could think of nothing else. At night, *Metroid* stopped my sleep. Unable to quell the need to finish the game, I became an insomniac once again. Blue light and periorbital darkness; an obsessive drive was writ round my eyes.

Against my resurgent *Metroid*-love, a dutiful counterpoint. To avoid indulgence I had to remain committed to the project of meaning. Remember—death is inevitable. Life is finite. To compensate, to keep myself on track, I started reading *Molloy*, the first of Samuel Beckett's *Three Novels*. Don DeLillo said Beckett was the 'last writer to shape the way we think and see.'[7] They say he changed what we mean by 'meaning.' Knowing this, I submitted myself for shaping. I wanted to be changed, impressed, improved. I desired a meaningful time.

Molloy, like its sequels *Malone Dies* and *The Unnamable*, is a ghost of a novel. The critics say it is a 'delicate drama of withdrawn consciousness,'[8] a novel about the 'totalitarianism of the inner world' where the body has failed and 'all that remains' is 'language.'[9] The first half is about a ruined man decaying into abstraction as he traipses through his hometown, his memory and mind failing him as he's endlessly diverted from seeing his mother. Throughout, the book teeters on the brink of meaning, babbling before the abyss. Neither the narrator nor the reader can say what is true or significant; they can only accept the flood of language.

Molloy is a great work; in Beckett's world, there is nothing but meaning. But despite its obvious appeal to someone like me, it was impotent next to my *Metroid*-love. Beckett and *Metroid*: their powers are incomparable. Every night when I would choose between them, I invariably reached for the latter. Against my game, Beckett had no authority over my consciousness. He put

---

[7]   *Mao II*, p.294.
[8]   *Against Interpretation*, p.4.
[9]   *The Savage God*, p.274.

me to sleep while *Metroid* kept me awake.[10]

The cult of value, the religion of purpose. Enjoying it more than Beckett, my *Metroid*-love eventually gave me the sense of guilt I thought I had escaped. When I stopped playing, the relief the game gave me ceased. The screen blackened and I remembered the inevitability of death. Choosing *Metroid* over *Molloy*, I had forsaken the meaningful for the purposeless, for something that lacks philosophical or intellectual insights, and which is empty of practically everything that makes for a strong, meaningful narrative. For nihilism manifest. I felt like I should be ashamed. Remember: I have thoughts about time. The idea of time, the passage thereof. The inevitability of death.

My mind said I should choose *Molloy* over *Metroid* and ordinarily, my guilt would've won the week. I would've chosen Beckett, and dutifully trudged through his endless paragraphs. But lately—blame the psychoanalysis—I've felt a little more courageous than usual. This time I didn't cow to the reprimands issued from my mind's superegoic heights. Instead, I decided I wasn't wrong to choose *Metroid*. No. Rather, I would defend my choice. It's what my heart desired, after all. So, better luck next time, Beckett. I like you, but I love someone else; I love *Metroid*.

---

[10] SOPORIFICS: Though this is not necessarily a criticism. Today, commenting on the sleep-inducing powers of art is occasionally phrased as a compliment. For some reason, people value art that helps them fall asleep. They praise its soporific qualities; maybe this is because their anxiety prevents them from sleeping. This accidentally savage compliment is often bequeathed to musical artists like the xx, Sigur Ros etc.

III
'An Erotics of Art'

Our problem: I pitted *Metroid* against *Molloy*, and *Metroid* won. Why? How? This is important. The reign of meaning is threatened. Remember the French writers, boy. *Tu es très existentiel, non?*

The answer is simple. *Metroid: Fusion* won because it is devoid of meaning, because it proves how meaninglessness is not the same as powerlessness. Far from it: instead, *Metroid's* shift away from meaning gives it more room to captivate us with emotion and desire. It has nothing else to work with, so it pushes these tools to their limit. A risky move, but the payoff is clear: by doing so *Metroid* gains the power to grip your consciousness. It acquires the ability to make itself unforgettable, unignorable. It can make you fall in love, in a way that words rarely can. In meaninglessness, *Metroid* somehow gains in significance.

Operating mostly outside language, *Metroid* works masterfully on the player's emotions and their sense of time, past, present and future. In the moment of play, it creates knots of fear so powerful that they can be recalled years later. At the right moments, it drives our anxiety to extremes, forcing its images to linger, preserved *Lepidoptera*-like, pinned into our cinereal architecture. Conducting our emotions, *Metroid* colonises the mind. In the present, it can dominate our perception; in the future, it haunts us, a spectre of pleasure once possessed; and in the past, in memory, it can set up immortal structures where others manage but a bivouac.[11]

---

[11] A PHILOSOPHICAL ASIDE: When I consider *Metroid's* mnemonic powers, Italo Calvino's words from *Invisible Cities* come to mind. 'Desires are already memories,' he says, yet memory 'is redundant: it repeats signs.' By this, he means, a) that our desires (by extension, our fears too) today are a form of memory, and b) our memory is itself the repetition of signs perceived in the past. Though he doesn't say so, in the absence

The critic of meaning may not think anything of *Metroid*. But for someone sensitive to the flows of desire, fear, love and memory—that is, for a critic who prefers affect to meaning—*Metroid* is a fascinating object.[12] Unlike Beckett, *Metroid* is an

---

of an alternative, we can assume that the repetition of signs is itself driven by desire. Calvino gives us a paradox, then—desire is self-sustaining, first using its power to encourage repetitions and memories, and then driving archaic desires back into being. *Metroid*—like the fantastical cities Calvino describes, and like so many other instances of great entertainment—plays on the closed loop of fantasy, emotion and repetition. *Metroid*, of course, is not something that inspired love, per se. Rather, its magic emerges from the way it manipulates our obsession and fear. It plays with the very Freudian notion that humans are compelled to repeat their traumatic moments: the idea that fear is a memory, a sign whose repetition is driven by terror. We try to remind ourselves of the dangers of our past, to steel ourselves against threats. Yet, we also hope to overcome this fear, to eliminate it entirely, breaking through it with our repetitive acts. *Metroid*—sadly unlike our real life—fulfils the fantasy that we might transcend our trauma and fear. Providing we're prepared to sacrifice enough of our delicate ear-hair follicles when he screams at us, we can beat Ridley-X,[a] procuring a sense of triumph and tinnitus for us, both being signs of the present form of a certain absence, i.e., said precious follicles and, if victorious, Ridley-X himself.

[a] GAMEPLAY TIP: Don't use diffusion missiles against Ridley-X; the charge beam will rip that fucker to shreds.

[12] SADO-MASOCHISM: This is possibly in part due to the basically sado-masochistic nature of the gameplay. Metroid, and games more broadly, have a unilateral ability to punish us, i.e., we can't punish the game, while they are usually designed so the player can eventually beat them. The player, to some extent, consents to being punished, in exchange for the effectively certain chance that we, with effort, will 'beat' the authority, the blunt-force-type connotations of this word being sounded here in full.

essentially non-hermeneutic artwork.[13] Its effects have nothing to do with the interpretation of meaning: *Metroid* is affective and emotional, but it isn't meaningful. And working without meaning and privileging emotion, *Metroid* is an almost perfect counterpoint to *Molloy* that succeeds in the way that the latter intends to. *Metroid* is an exact inversion of the modernist standard at its apogee in Beckett's work, and it moves us beyond words in a way that Beckett aspired (and failed) to: 'I don't know, that's all words, never wake, all words, there's nothing else....'[14] While *Molloy* is one of the last great modernist (or the first great postmodern) works, and while Beckett's *Three Novels* are an intense meditation on the meaning of meaning, *Metroid* forgets meaning entirely, and so becomes more radical, more memorable than *Molloy*.

Of course, *Molloy* and *Metroid* are works of different forms, each with its own particular strengths. But with its impressive manipulation of time, emotion and memory, *Metroid* presents a legitimate challenge to serious fiction, which, as any reader knows, is often concerned with memory, that other language of subjectivity. From Proust's magisterial colossus to Banville's work literature has burdened itself with innumerable meditations on our relationship to the temporal and the mnemonic. (Ironically, this renders most of them forgettable). Literature is littered with delicately wrought and hard-won insights on human memory: despite this focus, the mnemonic powers of video games

---

13   ON UNFORTUNATE TERMINOLOGY: For our purposes, 'hermeneutic' basically means 'interpretive.' John D. Caputo tells us in his *Hermeneutics* that the word is derived from the name of a Greek demigod, Hermes—i.e., in the same way that 'erotics' is derived from the god of love's name, Eros—whose job was to deliver messages between the mortals and the immortals. Hermes was variously depicted as a rogue and a helpful assistant, hence the need for an interpretation of his dualistic character, and the use of his name as etymological root for the name for the philosophy of interpretation.

14   *Three Novels*, p.407.

nonetheless exceed that of novels. While fiction often weaves beautiful, reflective filigrees via refined discussions of memory, and while these passages can be memorable, the simplest video game can sear itself into our minds. It is as though fiction understands memory, while video games *do* memory.[15]

Affectively and mnemonically, *Metroid: Fusion* is a more powerful work than most fiction. Beckett's *Molloy* included. Can we then say that *Metroid* is a better artwork than *Molloy?*

---

[15]   PHENOMENOLOGY: The discernible differences between the mediums allow games to more easily obtain this mnemonic power. Phenomenologically, video games have an unfair advantage, stimulating us on optical, aural, tactile, cognitive and affective levels. Books, however, are confined to the sight/intellect/emotion apparatus.[a] Compared to games, books rely on relatively minimal input from the other senses, so they have fewer avenues by which they can alter our affect and inspire our memory. Clearly, the forms are created unequal, and for this reason, it might be unfair to compare them. Putting aside these concerns, the fact remains: *Metroid's* images have lingered in the undergrowth of my unconscious, in the far reaches of memory, preserved as though enambered,[b] trapped in exact perfection, for over half my life, while few books have done the same. ('perfection is not of this world'[c] – sorry, you're wrong, Molloy.) When I was a child, *Metroid* provoked me to make memories, to wrap images in emotion and cinch them synaptically together in an unbreakable bond. *Metroid* was and is an utterly memorable experience, in a way that writing rarely is.

   [a] Though the universal, olfactory crispness of new books, and the musty smell of antiques are in some obscure way indispensable to our experience of the fiction they contain, as is the physicality of the book as object; I often remember passages both for their content and physical location on the page.

   [b] It turns out there is no generally accepted / widely used single word for 'trapped in amber'. *Collins Dictionary* gives us 'ambered', but I think adding the 'en 'prefix better gives us the meaning I'm after, as it comes out as 'within '+ 'amber', with the suffix telling us that 'amber 'here is a verb.

   [c] *Three Novels*, p.84.

Perhaps.[16] But no matter our opinion, my *Metroid* experience suggests there is merit to Susan Sontag's 1966 demand: 'In place of a hermeneutics', she writes, 'we need an erotics of art.'[17]

---

[16]   MNEMOGENICS: A perennial difficulty and generally fruitless and tedious exercise is the argument over the definition of 'great art'. As pretty much anyone can establish in a five minute conversation with pretty much anyone else, the potency of art is hopelessly a) intangible and b) subjective. Moreover, with Nietzsche, we've accepted that the death of God implies a dissolution of any singular interpretation of reality, meaning there is a literally infinite number of ways to approach this question and any piece of art.[a] While I certainly don't want to argue that the cognitivist/psychological perspective is final, exhaustive, correct, or even more useful than others, surely we can accept that an artwork's ability to inscribe itself on your mind, to structure our consciousness, to 'shape the way we think and see', is at least one indication of its greatness? Its capacity to provoke mnemogenesis—that is, the creation of memories—and to write itself into the fabric of our mind is certainly a measure of its power in at least one dimension. And if I consider that all my own favourite art has an immediate mnemonic potency, then perhaps we can say that this is a necessary, but not sufficient condition for an artwork's greatness?

[a] The 'multiplicity of interpretations' argument is strewn all throughout Nietzsche's books. But I've always liked aphorism 374 from *The Joyous Science* best: '... I think that nowadays we are at least far from the ludicrous presumption of decreeing from our corner that only perspectives from that corner are possible. On the contrary, the world has once more become 'limitless' to us, in so far as we cannot deny the possibility that it contains limitless interpretations.'

[17]   POLYTHEISM: I would add to her 'erotics' all other emotion-based modes of criticism we can think of. We could just as easily have called for a phobotics (fear), oizyotics (anxiety), deimotics (terror), or mnemonics (memory) of art, the Greek gods here being Phobos, Oizys, Deimos and Mnemosyne. In general, these would be more appropriate for *Metroid* than desire, with the

Sontag's call for 'an erotics of art' comes from her book, *Against Interpretation*, where she attacks the modernist critical establishment that she felt had privileged the intellect at the heart's expense for too long. In Sontag's eyes, the erotic, 'feeling' response to art had been repressed in the modernist period's critical discourse, leading us to become blind to art's most important aspect—not its meaning, but its 'pure, untranslatable, sensuous immediacy.'[18] Righteously dissatisfied and wanting to feel, she insisted we discard our taste for hermeneutics and embrace art in all its vivacious presence: to accept it for what it appears to be and how it makes us feel, rather than what we believe it means.[19] Against interpretation, Sontag says, we must allow ourselves to fall in love with art once more.

---

obvious exception of the moment where Samus steps out of her armour into aforementioned hot-pink bra + panty combo.

[18]   *Against Interpretation*, p.14.

[19]   SONTAG: In retrospect, it's clear Sontag was basically correct: we did need an erotics of art. After she published her essay, consumer demand for erotic, non-hermeneutic art quickly proved overwhelming. With a stroke of prescience and/or luck, Sontag identified the nascent, counter-cultural craving for artworks where 'feel' is more important than 'meaning,' a craving which remains strong today. Propelled by this desire, for decades creators in all mediums have enlisted our animal spirits in support of their vision; 20th century and contemporary art would be inconceivable without the elevation of the affective instinct, a.k.a. the replacement of the Christian God with Eros, a.k.a, what the Frankfurt School called repressive desublimation. To understand our culture today, we need to accept that porn is more popular than poetry. That our consciousness is shaped by artists whose primary medium is our desire. That art lives on the unrestricted flows of desire and emotion, liberated when we threw off the repressive authority of meaning. That it impoverishes us to interpret, say, David Bowie's '70s output,[a] or even less acclaimed art (take your pick: maybe, I don't know, the 1997 Bond film *Goldeneye*?[b]) in a purely hermeneutic light, and

that doing so is a basic misrecognition of the artistic project at hand. We also need to accept that, with the rise of popular erotic art, we didn't need Beckett to strip the novel bare, proving that its hollowed-out and ethereal form could still delight. While Beckett may have been the last writer to 'shape the way we think and see,' games like *Metroid: Fusion* inevitably perform a similar violence upon thinking and seeing creatures. Beckett is less shocking in a world where *Metroid* exists, precisely because the latter is both more powerful and less meaningful.

[a] BOWIE: If we take Bowie's 'All The Young Dudes' as performed by Mott the Hoople—especially the transition from pre-chorus (i.e. where the band moves through the chords Em^7-F#-Bm-A-G-A^7, absolutely hammering that dominant seventh at the end, where the singer—Mott, ostensibly, I've never checked—tells us: 'Television man is crazy saying we're juvenile delinquent wrecks/Oh, man, I need TV when I've got T.Rex/Oh brother, you guessed/I'm a dude, dad) to the chorus (i.e. where it resolves to a deftly ambivalent D major, with tones of melancholy, nostalgia, and passion while he says: 'All the young dudes / Carry the news!')—we can hear that the song's effects have a) literally nothing to do with the meaning of its words and b) are a result of basically every other element of the arrangement, performance, etc. From at least 1970 onwards, Bowie was an avid Nietzschean: this song is testament to the fact that God is dead, that the gods—Dionysus, Eros & Co.—have returned.

[b] BOND:[i] Incidentally, another game/movie franchise that has come up in analysis, Pierce Brosnan being an early masculine role model for me. The first outright ladykiller I idolised as a kid. *Goldeneye* gave me some strange feelings I now identify as my nascent sexuality. Gadgets, cars, suave with a dash of louche, unbearable sex appeal, and frequent sexual success. My analyst maintains the vital necessity of art as a prompt for psychological development. That an essentially sociopathic assassin was my hero is perhaps concerning.[ii] Whatever. All I can say is that I loved him: as a kid I wanted to be James Bond.

[i] BOWIE BOND: A nice metonymic coincidence: the Bowie Bond was a financial instrument created in 1997 by rock and roll investment banker David Pullman, that allowed investors to earn a return on the future sale of Bowie's catalogue, and whose value was equal to what investors gauged to be the present value of these expected future returns. Bowie used the proceeds from the sale of the Bowie Bonds to buy the ownership of his music, giving him full control over the licensing of his output.

Sontag's call for an erotics of art is ultimately a demand for memorable work; a mnemonics of art. As anyone who has loved can say, love and memory are inseparable; we rarely forget what we love. Once something is both loved and unforgotten, it persists within us. Through the amorous repetition of memory, love constantly works on our mind and body and restructures the way we see the world. Love is unforgettable, and our inability to lose our memory of love is partly what renders it a transformative force. Love—and equivalently, great terror—changes us; it is something we must endlessly react to. So, if we prize artworks for their power 'to shape the way we think and see,' then the importance of Sontag's argument for erotics and affect in art cannot be understated. Memories become most powerful when they collaborate with the heart; an intense, vital emotional response to a work can give it a mnemonic permanence and transformative potential that can't be achieved through its meaning alone. Being more readily memorised, affectively powerful works can revolutionise our minds in ways that merely meaningful works cannot. Erotics is more powerful than hermeneutics.

Unlike so much of the great fiction I have read, *Metroid: Fusion* is an utterly mnemogenic work: because it is so affectively powerful, it preserved itself almost wholly intact in my memory for over fifteen years. As a child and as an adult, *Metroid* forced me to respond, react—and above all, to remember. *Metroid* marked me indelibly, and for this reason alone it was able to surge

---

Despite this, the value of the bonds tanked pretty quickly, indicating that investors no longer believed in the capacity of the bond issuer to generate the expected return on investment, possibly due to his dire 1999 record *Hours*, and because Bowie didn't seem to be any good at generating profits with old material, relying throughout this period mostly on live records like *Bowie At the Beeb* and *LiveandWell.com*. At maturity, however, the bonds were repaid in full, thus presaging Bowie's ability to make a late-stage comeback, in spite of all expectations, as he did with his excellent death album, *Blackstar*.

[ii] Though, without endorsing any essentialist ideas, surely boys throughout history have grown up wanting to be like their favourite killers?

back into my life, provoking my obsession once again after a decade where it had lingered in memory. Both my original encounter with the work and my recollection of it inspired an intense surge of affect; each playthrough of the game was a transformative experience, and each time I recall it my emotions are transformed. In this way, I think, *Metroid: Fusion* is a superior piece of art and as a critic of erotics, I have to say that I prefer *Metroid* to *Molloy*. Shock. The reign of meaning is threatened.

IV
Life in the Grip of Significance

In psychoanalysis, we recently discussed a dream. It was basically an artless dramatisation of Sontag's hermeneutics/erotics conflict—a stageplay where a rational government crushed a political uprising, which represented the domination of affect by the intellect. This conflict, as it turns out, is one of my major symptoms. Like modernist critics, I also chose hermeneutics over erotics at one point, repressing my emotional life with a commitment to meaning.

In 2016, age 22, I had an encounter with major depression. Suicidal, a combination of sadness and nihilism nearly killed me: believing my life was meaningless despair, I felt I should end it. A modern affliction. Unable to manage the sadness myself, I tried instead to treat the nihilism. I never said it in so many words, but I believed I could think my melancholy into oblivion, believed that if I solved the problem of meaninglessness with meaning, I would save myself. Terrified of my irascible heart, I descended like one of Beckett's characters into a 'totalitarianism of the inner world' where there was nothing but words. There, I thought I would resolve everything through philosophical argument, the rational appeal. Oh, how much hope.

In this period I redoubled my devotion to the cult of value, the religion of purpose. Ensnared in words about meaning and death, infinite problems for infinite thought, I became a revenant in my own life. My inner world became so dominating I would walk into walls. All hermeneutics and no erotics, I couldn't see for all the words. I was a spectre, thick in the brush of meaning; an eidolon obsessed with *eide*. I lived in a 'strange world where I was a mere stray:' John Shade's 719th line. At one point, I felt Sartre was right: 'existence takes my thoughts from behind… somebody takes me from behind, they force me from behind to think … [like I am] raped by existence from behind.'[20] And after I bought a copy of Camus' *Myth of Sisyphus*, I took his words to heart—'there is but one truly serious philosophical problem and that is suicide…'[21]—and thought of my pain like a problem of logic, like an equation in need of a solution.

Years later, and after this habit was driven to an extreme when I was bullied at my workplace, I realised that being dominated like this wasn't normal; I now see I had developed a kind of addiction to thought. A dependence on the blood-rush of words. In my suffering, I wouldn't let myself forget to think. I had to remember to think.

Addiction: when I say this, I mean it literally. As I learned from *Infinite Jest*, 'addiction' is derived from the Latin *addicere*. Ad + dicere, literally meaning, 'to speak.' In its original sense, 'addiction' meant 'to devote one's life wholly' to something.[22] To give yourself and all your words away. Together, these ancestral facts tell us a little truth about the word. 'Addiction' doesn't necessarily concern drugs or any other substance. In its broadest sense, the word signifies a totalising commitment to a particular kind of speech: the panegyric, the praise-poem for the love-object. The addict can endlessly praise drugs or sex or thought or politics, or they can rhapsodise about video games or books. Irrespective of the object, though, the behaviour is the same. The addict's thoughts all lead to the same place; they speak endlessly about the same things. The addict devotes their life to a certain pattern of speech. Addiction. Ad + dicere. To speak.

---

[20] *Nausea*, pp.148–9.
[21] *The Myth of Sisyphus*, p.1.
[22] *Infinite Jest*, p.900.

After my dream, I talked about thought with my analyst. The sage burned, and we considered the irrational excesses of the rational mind. As I spoke and remembered, I realised I hadn't given myself to thought for philosophical reasons alone: my thinking was really a tool for self-protection against my chaotic emotions. Confronted with my ungovernable heart, I turned to thought with a perverse form of hope. Consciously, I hoped that with the right idea, I would dissolve the problem of nihilism and turn my sadness to vapour. But my anti-nihilistic pursuit was ultimately a distraction, and the content of thought was less relevant than its function: my real hope was to suppress my emotions with thought.[23] Though I believe that ideas had caused

---

[23]   THE SCHIZOID DEFENCE: It was during this conversation[a] that my analyst, for the first time in the six months since I started treatment, used a word with diagnostic connotations to describe my symptoms and experiences. That word was 'schizoid,' meaning, in the sense propounded by analysts like Harry Guntrip, someone whose personality is divided against itself, such that their desire for human relationships is deeply repressed, they fear their own desires,[b] and their emotions are disconnected from their intellect, leaving them predisposed towards solitary, often abstract pursuits, the content of which is often shaped by memories buried within the unconscious. People defined by the schizoid defence have a few archetypal traits,[c] but the antagonism between their rationality and emotions, and their taste for abstract intellectual pursuits that can be pursued in isolation, incl. but not limited to philosophy, metaphysics, literature, language, writing, and (probably) psychoanalytic theory, are most important for us.[d]

Feeling a rather powerful sense of identity with this description,[e] which made a constellation of my disparate sufferings and qualities[f] where for years I had only seen starsprent void, I did some research on the schizoid conditions after this session, and I found out that David Bowie exhibited schizoid traits, exemplified by his fixation on alien characters who have fallen to earth and now live out of joint with society, that more than a few critics think Beckett's fictions dramatize the schizoid condition, and that schizoid individuals are particularly susceptible to being bullied. I also discovered that Guntrip believed that existentialist philosophers from Kierkegaard to Heidegger to Sartre, whose work focuses on themes incl. anxiety, dread, nihilism, nothingness, meaninglessness, futility, uncertainty, and freedom, simply rationalised the 'schizoid despair' and loss of contact w/ emotional reality into a philosophical system, reifying / projecting it into an ontological condition instead of recognising it as a psychological and emotional phenomenon.

I also learned that the schizoid defence can emerge when an individual experiences an environmental failure that precipitates an extreme emotional response, leading them to flee from the external world into a realm over which they have greater control: that is, they retreat into thought. Severe failures of care in early childhood, e.g., neglect or sexual abuse, can inaugurate a habit of schizoid withdrawal, which can be reactivated in adulthood when said individual finds themselves trapped in abusive relationships, or becomes suicidal, or tries to work through profoundly difficult experiences buried in their unconscious, and responds to their pain by fleeing into abstraction or extended intellectual asides in a frantic attempt to write over their suffering with language.[g]

[a] Or was it a later one that repeated the same theme? I can't recall; within what André Green called the 'shattered time of the unconscious,' all blurs into an elongated present where the past is layered and refracts through itself; as I write and remember, I am having all these conversations, uncovering all these memories, simultaneously.

[b] Guntrip once used a lovely phrase to describe the schizoid individual's problem: he said that the schizoid's struggle is 'love made hungry,' or 'the fear of loving lest one's love or need of love should destroy.' The schizoid suffering stems from a fear of being both an object of desire and a desiring subject – in other words, it is a fear of relationality.

[c] I.e., in his *Schizoid Phenomena, Object Relations, and the Self*, Guntrip lists nine features that characterise schizoid individuals:

my sadness, thought was really an anaesthetic for me: it was a without-feeling that numbed me against tumultuous and untidy eruptions of feeling. Language was a narcotic, a substance to inspire numbness that I ingested with abandon and whose products are things like this book. I set myself impossible tasks and unsolvable philosophical problems to condemn myself to endless thought, and successfully distracted myself from my body, my emotions and the world outside. Numb and anaesthetised, I found myself in a world of hermeneutics without erotics. Life in the grip of significance. Shades of blood-black nihilism.

---

they are typically i) introverted / emotionally cut off from outer reality; ii) withdrawn; iii) narcissistic / intently focused on internalised love-objects, iv) self-reliant, in the sense that they disavow the need for human relationships, v) simultaneously lonely and deeply desirous of the human connection they reject, and who often vi) experience depersonalisation and sense that they lack a strong identity, vii) regress to earlier psychic positions, viii) maintain an imagined sense of superiority over others, and ix) appear affectless and unemotional to external observers. These traits often accompany symptoms of depression and anxiety, as well as a sense of emotional emptiness that are hypostasised as a sense of ontological meaninglessness, i.e., as philosophical nihilism.

d A description which, to my mind, sounds remarkably like Nieztsche.

e Which, I suppose, is evidence of my schizoid tendencies, in that I felt relief when I could name, and thus define, know and control, my emotions with language[i] (or, more charitably, of the comfort a diagnosis brings to someone suffering an unfamiliar illness, i.e., that knowledge brings to those faced with uncertainty.)

   i In a way, this made me a Foucauldian: as in *Discipline & Punish*, I used knowledge, discourse and language to confine myself, to discipline my disruptive parts, and to construct my subjectivity via domination.

f Incl. but not limited to depression, anxiety, nihilistic thinking, a simultaneous craving for / terror of relationships, sex and sexuality, an interest in philosophy, reading and writing, and a great discomfort with being desired and desiring others.

g That is, as I am doing right now, and have been doing throughout this essay, at a moment where I should be trying to *feel* rather than understand this shit.

My deference to thought, language and hermeneutics was not truly about meaning or nihilism. Rather, it fulfilled a repressive desire of mine; a move against feeling. Yet like all repressive movements, my obsession with meaning was marked by its opposite. My language addiction was born in a moment of terror where I desperately grasped at thought for security and safety. The habit remains marked by this traumatic birth: through negation, my thoughts were never free of emotion, and were defined entirely by feeling. Hermeneutics secured its dominant position in my life only by deferring to secret, higher emotions: terror, anxiety, dread.

In my life, I now see that meaning never triumphed over affect: my rationality was essentially irrational. I tried to become intellectual in my moment of terror, yet I remained primarily and ineradicably emotional. In retrospect, I also see that this solipsistic addiction was sustained not only by terror, but by pleasure too. Much like a substance addiction my fear-driven thought addiction was immeasurably pleasurable. I found great satisfaction in the act of making meaning, fitting flights of thought together. Though I lived in an atmosphere of pervasive fear, I received a libidinal payoff whenever I further tightened the knots of my thought. It was immensely pleasing to think, to bring an intellectual edifice of growing complexity from nothingness into the light, because I always got a little dopaminergic/serotonergic reward for my thought. Though its flashes of light were but the sparks of an overheating mind, cascades of heat spraying from frictional surfaces, my world of shade and flicker had an erotic appeal to it. My thought was sustained not only by fear, but by love—my addiction lived because it felt good, at least when compared to its alternative: confronting a life that had become emotionally untenable.

In my mind, that addictive labyrinth, contradiction and confusion reigned supreme. To suppress my emotions I genuflected to thought. But in doing so I created a sham safety; I worshipped a false god; I cultivated a false consciousness, and I did not eradicate fear or love within my world. I could only displace them, pushing them above and beneath myself, so they were, at once, both suppressed and supreme. In my supposedly intellectual world where I tried to shelter from my feelings, fear drove love, love drove fear, and purity, clarity and honesty were impossible: all my meaning remained entirely emotional. When I tried to render them inert, I made my emotions into a force that dominated my life. Oh, how much hope. How powerful, the need to protect the self.

My mind was a place of chaos because fear led me to prefer meaning to love. I tried to eliminate my feelings, yet they remained ineradicable because there was an erotic obsession with thinking about meaning at the heart of this repression. My intellect dominated my affect, yet it was propelled by my affect; my fear controlled my love, yet my fear found its power in Eros. And this turned me against practically all the culture I was weaned on. Towards *Molloy,* away from my humble *Metroid.*

This confusion is why I am in psychoanalysis at age 26. But in the process of untangling my mind, I provoked a return of the repressed. *Metroid: Fusion* symbolises all the emotion I subjugated and smothered with my thought: it is the whitecap on the flooding-in of affect, the foaming edge of the emotional storm-surge that is now sweeping into my world, that frozen land where meaning had prevailed at the expense of love for too long. Together, these feelings are a liberating force: with them, I can move from hermeneutics back to erotics. I can speak the language of the heartland I have neglected for so long.

V

The Symptom of Modernism

The return of *Metroid* shows that a primary psychological symptom for me is an echo of modernism. My suffering contains a re-enactment of the hermeneutics/erotics divide that dominated art throughout the modernist period. And my rediscovery of *Metroid* duplicates the earth-shattering moment where the erotic, countercultural movement displaced the earlier period's preference for meaning. In the 1960s when Sontag issued her demand, and in my own psyche as I replayed *Metroid*, Eros was unchained. Love and affect escaped the dominating regime of meaning and so transformed the world.

As with all re-enactments, my performance was not identical to the original. Artists like Brian Eno and philosophers like Gilles Deleuze tell us that repetition is a form of change. Though I restaged Sontag's movement from hermeneutics to erotics, I did so more than fifty years after she called for the same change and in a climate where I had already regressed from erotics. My context was different, so I had the chance to go beyond her thinking, see it from a new perspective, and understand its limitations.

Sontag said we needed an erotics of art in a world dominated by hermeneutics. She was correct, in a sense. But it seems that she misses something critical, because in my experience, the allegiance to meaning is secured by affect. To me, it seems that the dominance of hermeneutics could not have occurred without a more fundamental emotional attachment to meaning. What I see in my repetition, then, is the falsity of Sontag's dichotomy. We don't need hermeneutics or erotics. Rather, we need to understand that our preference for meaning is always an erotic/affective phenomenon, that desire and fear are entwined with meaning, and that erotics is essentially interpretive in nature. We need to see how meaning is never a solely linguistic experience: that the flood of language, the tumble of judgement, and philosophical thought itself are all totally emotional experiences.

Rather than continue with Sontag, and choose erotics over hermeneutics, I see that my language and my emotion must relate once more. They must be reunited. To do so, I must only see that the language spoken by a living being is always already suffused with emotion. Words are a vessel for the missives of the heart, affect which would otherwise remain trapped in private consciousness without language to bring it into the world. I also need to see that controlling emotion with language is an exercise in illusion and false consciousness, as the desire for control comes from the heart: the preference for hermeneutics sees the heart dominating itself with language. And, perhaps most importantly, I need to let the emotional tones of my language resonate loudly.

For this reason, I now see I was right to leave behind my *Metroid*-love. The pleasures of *Metroid* are undeniable. And I see that both it and other kinds of art can suspend the authority of hermeneutics and rationality, allowing us to flee meaning for meaninglessness, and to return to the former with new eyes. Yet it's also true that *Metroid* is hermeneutically unrefined and is incapable of providing the higher pleasures of art wherein meaning and love reinforce one another, their collaboration and opposition driving the work to profound heights. Despite these insufficiencies, I also see that I was right to choose *Metroid* over *Molloy*. Beckett's work rests at the very height of hermeneutic richness—and in occupying such a space, conjures up a powerful affective undercurrent of terror—yet his linguistic prowess ultimately elides and obscures its affective potential. A terror of death drives the language throughout Beckett's *Three Novels*, but this fear is repressed and subliminal, and is ultimately signified only by the flurry of language on the surface of his novels. Like the unconscious in psychoanalysis, we can uncover the latent emotion hidden in Beckett's words; yet because this emotional content can only be derived by implication, its effect for me is diminished.

Better than both *Molloy* and *Metroid* in my eyes is the art that directly relies upon the erotic encounter with hermeneutics. The writing that satisfies our craving for the affective intensity of meaning, rather than meaning itself. Ironically, then, it is the writing that drew me to my psychoanalyst in the first place that reveals the end goal of my analysis. In my favourite authors I find the synthesis of meaning and emotion that I must recognise to heal the split in my consciousness. With much of his writing, David Foster Wallace sought nothing as much as the emotional encounter with meaning. In his own words, he wanted to make his readers' 'heads throb heartlike': he wanted to sanctify 'the marriages of cerebration & emotion, abstraction & lived life' by using 'fiction's limitless possibilities for reach and grasp.' [24] *Infinite Jest* and short stories like 'Good Old Neon' achieve this with a dazzling power at times. Wallace plays at the limits of language; his prose can give the reader a near-religious experience of pleasure and meaning. It's all cerebral brilliance wrapped in full-bodied pleasure: it is both erotics and hermeneutics.

In this sense, Wallace follows Vladimir Nabokov—that other master, who may not have attributed as 'much individual genius' to Wallace's interests in 'competitive tennis, infinity, solipsism, and so on'[25] as we, but whose artistic project is similarly premised on the reader's erotic experience of meaning. Much of Nabokov's work relies on the elaboration of interpretive games. A reader of *Pale Fire*, *Lolita* or *The Gift* will miss a large proportion of its pleasure if they fail to engage with Nabokov's literary chess puzzles. But completing these games is not simply an intellectual enterprise; once the interpretive task in his novels is completed, not only does the reader feel the pleasure of solving a subtle literary puzzle, but they gain the pleasure of understanding Nabokov's system of metaphysics, aesthetics and ethics. Nabokov's success—measured by our memory of his works— attests to the power of his vision, and the essential correctness of his assumptions.

My favourite fiction is not merely hermeneutic or erotic. Instead, it overcomes Sontag's opposition and achieves an erotic response through meaning, and a meaningful experience through erotics. My passion for these works is not only emotional or intellectual: it is both. Now I understand this, I also see that it's true of other kinds of writing. If we accept that meaning and affect are irrevocably entwined and symbiotic then the source of the curious powers behind political writing and ideologies is

---

[24] From 'The Empty Plenum: David Markson's "*Wittgenstein's Mistress*" in *Both Flesh & Not*, p.74.

[25] FORESHADOWING: This is a quote from p.10 of *Lolita* that rather uncannily sketches out Wallace's major philosophical preoccupations seven years before this birth and a full thirty years before his first fiction emerged.

obvious: if emotion drives meaning, it also powers ideology. Hannah Arendt's *Origins of Totalitarianism* describes how terror drove the ideological thinking necessary to Hitler and Stalin's regimes. In Germany and Russia, fear propelled the masses' thought; the awful success of these regimes shows how effectively people can harvest terror-borne thought and writing for political ends. Similarly, the nihilistic logic that emerges in the minds of contemporary depressives—as Andrew Solomon writes, the pattern of thought wherein 'the meaninglessness of every enterprise and every emotion, the meaninglessness of life itself, becomes self-evident'[26]—is secured by the trenchant despair that runs phreatic within them, the turbid waters surging at their soul's edge. Their sadness delivers them to a paradox where they declare the meaningless of the world with language; their emotions lead them to believe that their words lack power, even as they insist upon the emotional significance of their conclusions. Against such nihilism—against myself—we must simply remind ourselves that theirs is an emotional argument; that meaning subsists so long as feeling lives within the world. And against the symptom of modernism, we must remember that every spray of language that smatters our mind bursts forth from both the head and the heart; the two can never truly be separated.

VI
Every Kind of Writing

When I first went to psychoanalysis, I was addicted to a certain kind of language. For years, I lived in the grip of significance out of the fear of meaninglessness. I thought I could only speak heartlessly of meaning; I thought I lived a hermeneutic life.

Through analysis—through memory, feeling and the combination thereof—I learned my beliefs were delusions. I discovered that I was not speaking a neutral, impartial language.

---

[26] *The Noonday Demon*, p.15.

I learned that this is impossible: that my words were suffused with fear and love; that they were secured by terror; that they thrived in that inverse world of lifelessness and lovelessness. Our words are always emotional and meaning does not exist without affect: the two are simply inseparable.

We cannot speak both truthfully and heartlessly. To write of a world without love or fear is a vast distortion, a scandal, and a grand lie: it is a cover-up of the highest order. If we want to speak truly of our lives, we need the freedom to pivot into every kind of writing, to remember all the languages that have affected and transformed us. Aligned with our hearts' motions, we must traverse the world of emotional languages—towards love, fear, anger, and sadness as we need—for it is only then that we can say honestly that we have not merely existed, but that we lived. Knowing this, we must accept the unity of language and feeling, and allow our words to reach our hearts once more.

Every week I move closer to a world where I can speak meaningfully and emotionally; where my words spring from the head and the heart at once. Having lived in exile for so long, I don't know what this coming world is like. But I suspect and hope it is one where I will find freedom in feeling, language and action, along with the unity all three. I believe I approach a multilingual life where I can speak any and all rational, emotional languages and indulge in every kind of writing; where I will find the freedom to remember, feel, speak and think. I think I am opening upon a world of hope. Psychoanalysis seeks nothing less than this freedom; today, after my encounter with *Metroid*, the return of my lost love, I believe that it will deliver. [27]

---

[27] FOOTNOTES: And what about these footnotes? Were they a fearful distraction from the main text, the working-through of difficult feelings? Were they necessary? Were they both at once – a way of returning to the heart via the head?

The Enjoyment of Negativity:
On *The Social Dilemma*

I
God Isn't Dead, He Lives in Silicon Valley

AT THE MERCY OF WHATEVER obscure algorithmic forces dictate our lives, in 2020 many of us watched the Netflix film *The Social Dilemma*. Enraptured by our irascible gods—postmodern deities whose digital powers make a mockery of self-determination, autonomy, free will, the Enlightenment project at large, etc.— we all consumed a film wherein tech evangelists proselytise for approximately 90 mins about the evil technologies they created. Supposedly reformed, these defectors—the Righteous Reborn— sound a unified clarion call: Big Tech is our Present Disaster, they say, and they are here to help us Fix the Fabric of Democracy. An admirable goal: however, the film ironically and unwittingly condemns its subjects. Not only do the filmmakers fail to show the subjects apologising or expressing remorse for their behaviour: they make them look more like tragic and repulsive Dostoevsky characters than the saints they are supposed to be.

II
Dostoevsky in San Francisco

Much like social media designers themselves, *The Social Dilemma* relies on various techniques of manipulation. Of these, one is especially obvious. All good documentaries employ a covert narrative structure, and *The Social Dilemma* is no different. It relies on yet another repetition of a naïve story and like Instagram's behavioural modification techniques it's invisible but effective.

The Social Dilemma presents a tale of knowledgeable accomplices/ignorant pawns who unwittingly participated in a project of great harm, realised the errors of their ways and now want to do good. After working for Big Tech, the interviewees realised their mistakes, and now wish to redefine themselves as activists. Crusaders for The Good. Canaries in data-mines.

This narrative structure ought to be familiar to every viewer of modern entertainment and all those who have read Dostoevsky's *Crime & Punishment*: we know it as the Redemption Arc. It's a familiar story that we immediately recognise in *The Social Dilemma*, which gives us a coterie of recovering tech entrepreneurs/employees who are currently on the acclivitous slope of a steep moral climb. The Redemption Arc has many uses and here, the filmmakers employ it in its most naïve form: they deploy it to give the film Moral Authority and to encourage us to trust its subjects. The film—and, presumably, the Righteous Reborn—need us to believe they are The Good Guys. But can the viewer trust these people?

To put it bluntly, my answer is a resounding No. In truth, I barely know where to begin with the failures that undermine the authority of this film. Maybe its central ironies will do.

It doesn't take much insight to see that *The Social Dilemma* capitalises on our fear of social media, and generates more profits and information for the industry criticised in the film by doing so. That the film's existence shows how our fear of social media has been commodified by companies that practise surveillance capitalism; that such companies designed it and promoted it to us by using their information on our personal preferences; that viewing this film gives them even more information about our tastes, specifically concerning our enjoyment—yes, enjoyment— of our fear and paranoia about social media; that the film's popularity, partly induced by promotional algorithms, guarantees that the companies we fear will create more products that play with this fear; that the film's existence demonstrates a central problem of today's capitalism, i.e., how it has a remarkable ability to profit from both endorsements and attacks and can nullify and commodify critical voices while reinforcing profits; that *The*

Social Dilemma reveals that negativity is a form of entertainment, and that negativity about entertainment is also a form of entertainment; that, as interviewee Jaron Lanier says, 'it's the critics that drive improvement' in our consumer societies.

Any of these would be good starting points. But to me, these complaints are less salient than the neutered social criticism on display in the film. Most saccharine are the film's vague appeals to Fix the Fabric of Democracy Itself.[1] These days, we all know that Democracy is gravely threatened; nothing is so banal as the millionaire's anxiety about the loss of Democracy. But in *The Social Dilemma*, as in real, contemporary America, the anxious have no truly political solution to this problem. In the film, Fixing Democracy encompasses a narrow spectrum of options. We can change our demands as consumers—Tristan Harris, millionaire and ex-Google employee, appeals to the miserable democracy of the free market for his solutions, and asks that 'we demand that these products be designed humanely,' without considering how humaneness necessarily occupies a secondary position for corporate product designers operating in capitalist free markets— or we can ask our governments to impose regulations on Big Tech to make them Less Bad.[2] Yet as the interviewees are aware, our

---

[1]   I exempt Shoshana Zuboff from this criticism; her arguments for completely outlawing the markets for human attention are a moment of respite from the rest of this film.

[2]   With the abundant use of Democracy as symbol in this film and our cultural production at large, critical viewers are bound to notice the presence of certain patterns in the representation of our most cherished political ideal: that is, appeals to democracy always point us towards a rather disappointing and conservative political praxis. Once again, Slavoj Žižek is the critical voice *par excellence* here, writing that Democracy is 'today's main political fetish.'[a] In his Lacanian-Hegelian parlance, Democracy is the 'sublime object' of contemporary liberal political ideology. Essentially, this means that our ideal does not exist in immanent reality; it's an abstract concept, so we can only appreciate

governments are beholden to Big Tech's massive powers—
powers that only exist because the government chose not to
intervene earlier, preferring instead to let Silicon Valley
entrepreneurs accumulate private wealth and political influence.
Regulation is almost certain to be ineffective as our regulators
have already been bought by the subjects of regulation. The film
says nothing of this problem, and its solutions all aim at
conserving private power.

Conforming to prevailing political discourses, some
interviewees also lament the fact that our media environment
erodes objective, shared truths. But again, this insight is nothing
novel. Indeed, this objection was raised years before Facebook
went public by none other than David Foster Wallace. In 2005,
he said that the media's oligopolistic market structure, coupled
with its plurality of (often conservative) stations whose reporting
is explicitly ideological, had produced 'a situation of extreme
fragmentation' and 'the kind of relativism that cultural
conservatives decry, a kind of epistemic free-for-all in which "the

---

democracy as it manifests in our real political world, once it
becomes a 'miserable, radically contingent corporeal leftover' of
our grand idea.[b] We must examine democracy as it really exists
and in doing so, we see that *The Social Dilemma*'s vision of
democracy is one where democracy is inert and inactive. The film
presents no policy ideas outside of increasing regulations on Big
Tech, despite the fact that this is a woefully inadequate solution,
and that better and more radical solutions, such as public
ownership of social media and the creation of a human right for
data sovereignty are well-known today. They want a democracy
without power for people, and where corporate authority is
basically preserved. We shouldn't hope for the radical change we
need if *The Social Dilemma*'s ideas are the limits of what we will
accept as a solution.

[a] *Welcome to the Desert of the Real!*, p.78.

[b] *The Sublime Object of Ideology*, p.234.

truth" is wholly a matter of perspective and agenda.'[3] Fake news and the death of truth were here before Twitter. We simply needed platforms that could profit from the anxious discourse on fake news for it to awaken within mainstream political consciousness. Had The Righteous Reborn heeded Wallace's warning, they could have avoided the situation they have created.

When the Righteous Reborn tell us they couldn't have predicted How Bad Social Media Would Become, we must at least partly believe them. No matter their goals at the outset of their projects, they could never have foreseen the extent of their success and damage. Yet while the degree of the harm caused was beyond prediction, the nature of the damage they inflicted is precisely what they should have expected. Each of our Righteous Reformed worked for companies whose stated *raison d'être* was to generate profit by a) creating products that would hyper-drive the existing principles of surveillance, advertising and addictive product design, and b) inflict these products upon billions of people. They sought nothing more than a version of 20th-century capitalism heightened to the point of hysteria. Despite this, the film is silent about capitalism's broader advertising industry, which has relied on surveillance, behavioural alteration, and manufactured dependency for decades, and of which social media is simply the apotheosis.

Our Righteous Reformed, much like their former employers, also claim that they didn't foresee the mental health effects of their enterprise. Billionaire developer Justin Rosenstein states he only wanted to spread 'positivity and love' when working on Facebook's like button—that is, the feature that undergirds the platform's violently stratified social ecosystem and its rapacious marketing apparatus, and which has ethical indifference as a core feature, consumers being capable of expressing support for any kind of message with it, be it positive and loving or hateful and bigoted. Their lack of clairvoyance is similarly disheartening. As

---

[3]   See
https://www.theatlantic.com/magazine/archive/2005/04/host/3
03812/

we learned from 20th-century totalitarian states like Soviet Russia and Nazi Germany, mass surveillance is the basis for perpetual terror. It forces rigid conformity and creates a culture of pervasive scrutiny among its subjects, who start to autonomously enforce the oppressive norms. Under surveillance people become fearful. Doubtful. Trust, the basis of the Fabric of Democracy, is destroyed, leading to loneliness, uncertainty and higher rates of mental anguish. Unsurprisingly, suicides increase in such circumstances. We know this: had the interviewees been aware of history or cared to listen to its messages then the psychological effects of their products would have been totally predictable. Even worse than the historically ignorant are interviewees like Tim Kendall, Facebook's first Director of Monetisation and a key developer of their advertising business, who prohibits his own children from using the products they designed. 'We are zealots… we're crazy,' he says, 'and we don't let our kids have any screen time.' The quiet admission of guilt here is crushingly loud.

The problems that the Righteous Reborn mention—or neglect to mention—are not new. Yet they are content to insist, again and again, that the Present Disaster is some *sui generis*, never-before-seen type of shit. We don't know whether this lacuna is the fault of the film's editors or its subjects. Nonetheless, it's a gaping hole in this apparently radical exposé that substantially reduces the credibility of its interviewees. Indeed—it makes their claims to ignorance look like an excuse. Like a sign of guilt, hidden and repressed. Like they're unsure if they have achieved redemption.

Ultimately the film's Redemption Arc fails, and it's because the Righteous Reborn remind us of Dostoevsky's more ambivalent characters. In David Foster Wallace's words, Fyodor was one of the first writers 'to understand how deeply some people love their own suffering, how they use it and depend on it.'[4] In novels like *Crime and Punishment*, Dostoevsky's drama

---

[4]   Footnote 14 from 'Joseph Frank's Dostoevsky,' in *Consider the Lobster*, p.264.

relies on the religious notion that we can draw tremendous masochistic pleasure from guilt and apology. Dostoevsky knew we can produce pathos for ourselves by first becoming a criminal and then a penitent. He knew that we love to make ourselves the subjects of guilt and redemption.

I suspect our Righteous Reborn are sensitive to this notion. After pursuing immorality with total abandon they sacrificed their economic profits for surpluses of the heart. Acting with pure negligence, they created the grounds for their redemption; then they performed it and reaped the pleasures of self-renunciation. The sweetness of repenting. The joy of condemning yourself in the eyes of a higher authority. Of lashing themselves at the feet of their gods to restore their goodness. Really, the interviewees are like Raskolnikov. They are people who produced their own guilt, only to harvest the pleasure that comes with its relief. The Righteous Reborn spent their lives building the redemption narrative *The Social Dilemma* relies on and then they capitalised on it. No matter what they gained, the cost of this story is obvious. Years of moral blindness were required before they could feel like truly moral actors. To attain redemption they had to first create damnation.

Readers abhor Raskolnikov's hypocrisy and for the same reason, I admire neither the bravery nor the supposed self-sacrifice of the interviewees. It's good that their ethical consciousness has finally emerged from its coma, its sleep-state bought by the narcotic cocktail of dollars and ideology. Yet the fact remains: they all allowed themselves to participate in obviously damaging practices for years. Even worse, their dissent earns them a nice profit, public recognition and unanimous social approval: these people have transitioned from being a) well-compensated IT technicians and entrepreneurs to b) high-profile activists who speak on an international platform owned by other Silicon Valley entrepreneurs (i.e. Netflix), and so retain their privilege and remain within the system they apparently oppose. Fundamentally their shift was a safe and self-serving move. To me this means they are not heroic. Rather, they have simply grown the appearance of moral mediocrity after living in a state where their ethical sensibility was hideously underdeveloped; their virtue is ill-fitting as consequence.

Most disingenuous, then, are the claims that these men only wanted to spread The Good with their technological projects: connection, love, communication, and so on. From the moment that they began work in hyper-competitive, utterly capitalistic Silicon Valley, they knew precisely what they wanted to achieve. They desired power, dominance, and private profits. They hoped to be masters of the universe, tragic gods. They sought the drama of redemption. That there is little trace of The Good left in the products they willingly designed while they remain prodigiously wealthy and socially prominent ought to show them that The Good was never their primary aim. Otherwise they would have bothered to protect it. With this in mind, my overall feeling for *The Social Dilemma* is one of contempt. The film's title gives it all away: we only face a dilemma because those who hold positions of power in our society have not a shred of integrity within them.

Maybe we ought to be a little forgiving: it is easy, after all, to confuse Profits with Benevolence in today's economy. But if we accept that our present Social Dilemma was the result of such confusion, we must pause to consider the nature of our society. For this would mean that our most intelligent people are utterly clueless about ethics, empathy and compassion. It would mean that the most powerful people in the most powerful society ever are bereft of even a mediocre moral compass. If this is the case, then we ought to be far more concerned about the fate of our world than even *The Social Dilemma* suggests.

Holding Patterns: or, the Terror of Communication

I
Nothingness

IF I REMEMBER CORRECTLY, and I'm not *sure* that I do, my earliest memory of a Mass Media Event is from September 11, 2001 – the day the Twin Towers fell. As the towers collapsed, I fell into world-history; I was dragged into time by terror communicated through TV and newspapers.[1] On that day I learned of the flux and fall of empires through images and media. Discovered the violent potential of time. The terror of communication.

My memory goes like this: I am seven years old, in class, second grade, pondering the trailer for the upcoming *Spiderman* film,[2] sitting next to my friend who may be doing the same. Townsville, Australia. September 12th, 2001. 15,480km from Ground Zero. After the fact but still unaware. Waiting to start our lesson. The teacher arrives. The teacher sits down. Her face tense like she's suppressing distress. A quiet moment, then she holds up a newspaper.

I don't remember the headline. But I can't forget the front-page picture: blue sky and grey buildings disturbed by hell-red. Steel swallowing steel in a smoking bloodburst, a haemorrhage of energy. A Kantian act of violence, tearing open the world's façade to reveal the in-itself inferno that roils beneath it all. The planes hit the buildings and ripped an arterial split in reality. Now the planes and the buildings and all the people trapped inside were

---

[1] This doesn't make me unique: it's a cultural phenomenon, the birth rite for children born between maybe 1993 and 1995.

[2] See https://youtu.be/Ozz8uxW733Q

gone. New York, NY—a place I only know from TV shows—weeps for their loss.[3]

As a child this adult event is beyond my understanding. I had never even seen a skyscraper in the flesh, never felt the inverse vertigo inspired by the sublime, the human scale approximating nothing when standing beside the gigantic. Quietly disturbed, I lack the language for this collision of world and heart. I feel a deep uneasiness; an obstruction between my child-lungs and child-mouth. Something had gone wrong in those obsidian hollows behind language, the caverns upon which thought is built, from which words emerge. I look at the floor, out of joint with my own body. I say nothing. Speechless for the fact that unspeakable violence was possible.

My friend is not beset by such ambivalence. He probably thinks it is a still from a Hollywood film. He had seen it and loved it all before; unashamed of his pleasure, he shouts his approval.

'That's so cool!' he says, in awe of the image.

My teacher recoils, moderately horrified.

'This is real,' she says.

That day my teacher was correct: the image was real. Like a movie, like a memory, the picture entered the room and our child-minds where it had a real effect. It warped the atmosphere; it cracked our consciousnesses, 9/11 was as true to him, to her and me as any event or film we had seen.

I still don't know what to feel about the image or the event. But now, in memory, I feel a sympathy for my teacher and my friend. She was right to be horrified and he was right to be amazed: the spectacle was both awesome and terrible, hideously surreal and violently true. And obviously my friend's enthusiasm was not for the Al Qaeda cause: his passion was secured by his

---

[3] Another famous image I saw later that day. A man sailing headlong into negative transcendence: his bent knee disrupts the Cartesian plane behind him, the modernist grid perpendicular to the one on the ground; his billowing shirt hints at the abyss; he is a skydiver, a skywriter, that presages the building's fate. And from him, I learned of suicide.

child-love for the nihilistic technology that erases the boundary between the false and the true, the artifice and the real, entertainment and terror, turning our world into entertainment and making entertainment our world; for his uncensored indulgence in the pleasures of horror.

Unlike my teacher I don't think we can fault my friend's excitement. To me it seems that he understood media better than her: her reality principle was outdated. He knew that the potential of print and television was the sublime, painted in shades of fear and awe. And in 9/11, those pictures and words that disfigured our fear, our memory, our language—that is what he got. With terror, the suicide pilots created a *sui generis* media event. They violently kicked in the boundaries of news, entertainment and art, and they ushered in a new aesthetic: with their architectural violence, they taught us an entirely new pattern language.

With 9/11, the terrorists achieved what most entertainers can only hope for: they gave us true novelty. And this young boy, a lover of spectacle, responded as he had been conditioned. His passion was for the avant-garde; he sought the unseen. To be moved—that was his *raison d'être*. Naturally, the violence of 9/11 left my friend wild with desire. He enjoyed the arrival of death's dream kingdom. Readied by television, he was prepared to speak whatever language terror demanded of him; he could say the words most were too polite, too horrified of themselves to say. When the moment arrived, he opened his mouth and the dark lights burning within lunged out.

II
Power

'I think if you maintain a force in the world that comes into people's sleep, you are exercising a meaningful power.'
—Don DeLillo, *Underworld*, p.76

'...in a society that's filled with glut and repetition and endless consumption, the act of terror may be the only meaningful act... People who are powerless make an open theatre of violence.'
—Don DeLillo, interviewed in *The New York Times*, May 19, 1991

'True terror is a language and a vision. There is a deep narrative structure to terrorist acts, and they infiltrate and alter consciousness in ways that writers used to aspire to.'
—Don DeLillo, interviewed in *The New York Times*, May 19, 1991

III
The Ground of Being

True terrorism has always been a physical violence; in our modern world it is also a traumatic communicative act, disseminated through world media; it is a language event that births its own ambivalent poetry.

When we witness an act of terror, it makes a paradoxical demand of us. It says: 'Whereof one cannot speak, thereof one must *not* be silent.' Terrorism inscribes a crack upon our minds that forces us to speak and leaves us speechless; in violence a fissure is written in us that both demands and resists representation. Terror is beyond, beneath or above meaning; it is out of time with language, too early or too late for words. Yet sadistically, it asks that we make meaning of it.

Terror thus inflicts a loud, silent secret upon us: like the idea of God or a forgotten trauma, it gives us an unspeakable truth we are compelled to share. Violence fills the blue air with strange words: it drives us into a holding pattern of unsuccessful speech, thought and interpretation, into an automatic language that fails the task of signification. (Repeat, repeat, inch closer to the receding Real.)

With time, our frustrated compulsion and failed repetitions become a practice that teaches us to think and hear; our fear forms the ground of a certain knowledge, a new way of (mis)understanding things. Eventually terror becomes the origin-point for our beliefs, the God of our dark hopes and light dreams, the centre of our being. Operating both on and through speech, it obliterates what we once were and reforges us anew.

Terror is a language that both destroys us and creates us. It is a drama of possibility and impossibility that anchors our babble, shapes our minds and shackles our actions. Terror alters the meaning of our words and world; it is a deathbirth that endlessly changes us.

Every act of terror brings us a new language, a new way of being. To me, 9/11 is an exemplary dialect of the language of terror. The day redefined my being and made me a paradox: with 9/11 I became a person who needs to speak of something beyond language, a rambling aphasiac for whom words are necessary and insufficient. (How can the living speak of so much death? How can we represent the truth of something that will only ever be a representation to us?)

From the moment it arrived in my life, the tempest of the event was fixed firmly in the past. It was always-already signified; my fear was for images. Yet its swirl of words still disturbs me; for when I absorbed the signs of this unspeakable moment in time I did not witness in a city I have never seen, my thoughts were rewritten in terror's language. The visions of terror crash-landed in my mind, and amid the debris scattered among the silent spaces within me, they started to murmur their poetry. I listened, I practised, I became fluent in its fractured vocabulary; through time I became terrorised.

Sometimes I think I know the perverse secrets of this language; at other times I think I know nothing. Perhaps these are the same thing. Either way, the language of 9/11 inflicts a strange blend of power and impotence upon its speakers. At once it inspires tremendous, imaginary fears within us while it leaves us unable to speak of our visions in any meaningful way. 9/11 makes us feel impossible, insufficient and unstable. It commits us to infinite fearful thought where we babble broken words; it makes our words meaningless and necessary. Surely the terrorists knew it would have this disquieting effect: I imagine it's why they created the spectacle.

I don't know if we can settle on our interpretation of 9/11. Forever we may be terrorised by our memory of the day and the repeated experience of words that fail to signify the violence. But perhaps we can escape this perverse dynamic if we create a soothing fiction that explains our inability to interpret. If we discover the story of our loquacious wordlessness, maybe we can conclude our labours in the language of terror. Or maybe not; hopeful yet hopeless, here we go.

Our inability to articulate this terror probably has several causes; foremost is the general inadequacy of words to their task. The gap between language and its referents, the freeplay between the event and its banal signifier, '9/11',[4] always compromises our attempts at meaning. I accept this, yet I venture another hypothesis that I believe is more specific to the event. Perhaps I don't know what to make of 9/11 because there is nothing to make of it; maybe, I can't understand it because of its nihilistic nature.

An abyss writ upon the sky: 9/11 was an impossible terror that confronted us with the thought of nothingness. For a Western child like me, 9/11 was a genuinely nihilistic moment: it turned something into nothing, it annihilated meaning and left us with

---

[4]   Why didn't we attach the year to this epithet? Its absence implies abstraction, a lack of anchoring: untethered to any specific 9/11, bound to 9/11 in general, a certain eternality and timelessness attaches to the day. The name itself prepares us for repetition…

empty space. In its wake, we had to speak of the event, so we had to find a way to positively represent this negativity. This meant we had to depict nothingness with something, to show absence with presence; we needed to create the destroyed, to tell a story about nothing.

But labouring beneath the injunction of the day's violence, we discovered that there is no positive image of nothing; we cannot create one without distorting the thing we have to represent. And so we failed when we tried to speak of this terrible day: there was nothing to say, but we could not and cannot say it.

9/11 was a moment of awful negation. Despite its nihilism— or perhaps, because of it—the terror nonetheless carried great meaning. The event was a burst of meaninglessness with a 'meaningful power'. It was beyond meaning, yet it infected our dreams and our words; it destroyed meaning while forcing it into existence. Incredibly significant but beyond signification, 9/11 was an aporia: it was something we had to speak of in a language of meaninglessness. It gave us a logical impossibility; our failure to speak, then, is the event's true signifier.

By demanding the impossible 9/11 crippled our means of interpretation: permanent hermeneutic failure is its true psychic damage. 9/11 opened us to the void and immured us in nihilistic language where meaning lives and dies at the same time, where our words reach for nothing and fail. It made us fear the unknown and our ignorance, the dark realms from where everything and nothing can spring. To quell our terror, we tried to repress our fear and ignorance with our cracked, nihilistic language; we tried to understand, to tell ourselves a satisfying story. We failed, and the terror remained; afraid, we would try again. With Beckettian irony, we would fail again. Fail better. Or better worse.

Playing these failed games of language, narrative and memory, we changed who we became. Through repetition I developed an obsession over what was not present, and I started to dread the absent, the yet-to-come, the horrible possibility. As a distant witness to an atrocity I came to know an empty fear of things removed in space and time; of things that, strictly speaking, did not exist outside my imagination. The erasure of the boundary

between the false and the true, the artifice and the real: immured
in a dust-cloud of dread dreams sweeping the cities of my mind,
I became afraid of nothing, of nowhere, of nobody.

(I also discovered the quiet, masochistic pleasure of perennial
terror; that our limitless anxious language is its own endless
entertainment; that we are never bored when there is nothing to
fear, when we forever inflict powerful reminders of our weakness
on ourselves.)

To be afraid of nothing; this is a most human madness. To fear
what is not and may never be requires the creative, spectral
genius only our species possesses; we need the imagination for
infinity and nullity, lack and abundance, God and death, the
logics of ∞ and ø. The phrase's insanity is betrayed in its rich
linguistic ambiguity: if someone says they are afraid of nothing,
they can mean they are not afraid, that there is no cause for fear
or that they fear nothingness itself. My terror-anxiety combined
the latter two fears: 9/11 was an eruption of nothingness
signifying how erasure could arrive from nowhere at any time; it
also gave me the fearful thought that this could happen to me—
that I too could be erased.

As its nihilistic images were communicated through the
media, 9/11 inscribed a fear of two forms of nothing on my mind;
there they began to harmonise, vibrating and combining. Because
ours is an atheistic society, I quickly heard how this poetry
matches another kind of terror that resounds in our godless
minds: it matches our fear of death. Heidegger once wrote that
objectless anxiety concerns 'nothing and nowhere.' [5] Lacking
place and substance, he concluded that the fear of nothing's real
object was the annihilating death that awaits us in time—the
nothingness beyond the edge of life. My fear of negation and
imagined absence, then, is little more than a fear of my inevitable
dissolution. My terror-fear is identical to my death-anxiety: both
focus on nothing.

In the wake of the skywritten annihilation and the event's
violence upon our language, I drew the triple thought of death,

---

[5]   *Being & Time*, pp.186–7.

nothingness and the absent—they are really the same thing—
deep into myself. Nestled at the core of my world I repeated it
like a hymn, murmuring my death-words. Nothingness became
the organising fiction of my life; I believed in the power of the
absent and became constantly conscious of death—existentially
authentic, in Heidegger's eyes.[6] In my authenticity and with my
empty words, I anxiously worshipped the terrible power of
nothingness, and I thought death embodied its darkness. I
believed nothing awaited us on the other side of life and that
terror would push me into the dark maw, the synaptic null, the
atheistic abyss beyond the border of being.

In other words: 9/11 made me a nihilist. Terror united fear
and nothingness in me, and led me to believe in the nihilistic
fiction.[7]

All this; the ambivalent poetry of terror. Like DeLillo
predicted, terrorism was a meaningful act in our society: 9/11
was a violence against identity and imagination; a crime against
being and becoming that rewrote our beliefs and our languages.
It gave us a new kind of God.

That day, violence burned nothingness into the sky; in the
light-shadow of absence, the emptiness was multiplied *ad
infinitum* in the media; absorbing the images of nothingness, we
fell into indeterminacy and learned a failed language we had to
use for an absurd necessity—to symbolise what could not be
symbolised.

In the days and years afterwards, we repeated our impossible,
paradoxical task, endlessly re-terrorising ourselves and filling our
minds with failed nothings. This practice taught us about the
simultaneous power and impotence of language; with our
meaningless words, we learned to fear the absent, to dread

---

6   Ibid, pp.289-92.
7   But doesn't this mean that I have failed again? Haven't I
     universalised a certain fiction of nothingness and collapsed the
     boundaries of fiction and reality to explain the
     incomprehensible? Yet isn't this the only way we can overcome
     our trauma—through insufficient stories?

negation and death. Maybe we even excavated some pleasure, some entertainment from our anxiety.

Through insistent impossibility and traumatic necessity, through entertainment, the loud, silent secret of 9/11 is now written within us all. The event's impossible reality, its unbelievable truth is that it is a meaninglessness with 'meaningful power'. 9/11 is nothing yet it is significant; we can find its meaning in the weakness of language and the power of nothingness. After 9/11, we discovered our words mean nothing and nothing means everything. Terrorised into nihilism, our lives are now built in the umbra of nothingness; so darkened, we have all changed how we die and how we live.

IV
Phenomenology & Ethics

After 9/11 my perception changed; the day traumatised my interpretations. The world's light now bent through smoke and sundered windows; I dreamed of new, terrifying futures; fixated on the violence of public spaces.

In the great junkspaces of modern society, I overlaid everything with images of random violence, with footage from TV. In airports and stadiums I fastidiously envisioned men in dark clothes, death exploding from the air itself. Always the masculine. At the shopping mall I saw polished tiles cracked by gun fire, their gaps a grid of veins. Visions of marble coursing with blood pumped from blasted bodies; identical white isles in a carmine sea. An imperial rouge on austere white; a few ounces of blood diverted from their natural channel.[8]

As a child these were my daydreams, my entertainment, my fantasies in the peace of sleep. These dread reveries taught me how to live; they gave me rules of the self, an ethics articulated in words of fear that were not really mine.

---

[8]   See David Hume's *Of Suicide.*

When I was twelve years old, there was a dress rehearsal of my terror-ethics; my family and I were evacuated from an airport.[9] News archives confirm my memories that hardly seem real today. I read the article and the day returns. (How convenient, how troubling that the cracked dreams that live in our minds are eternally preserved as media events, as entertainment and communicated terror.)

The evacuation begins when authoritative voices fill the air, telling us to calmly leave the terminal. When I hear this disembodied God-speech, I disconnect, and derivative daydreams instantly arrive. A bullet shattering my occipital bone. Klaxons wailing, brains spilling onto the floor, blood spreading cartographically. With dead eyes, watching my family following: facedown, crack, *fin*. Visions for the exodus, for the transmigration of souls. A film for departing the terminal; for the terminal departure.

My mother grabs my arm and ruptures my reverie. We then do as the voice commands. We begin to move. To my young mind, both petrified and excited, we must be leaving the airport because terrorists are coming. Nobody tells me otherwise so I think what I am conditioned to think. Metal detectors cry their staccato babble, their electric threnody, as we exit the airport to sit on the bitumen outside.

My body is strangely serene under an abstract sun, where we wait for over an hour. As I sit on the hot pavement, the light lancing through data-dense skies, I imagine my death a thousand times. Repetition and trauma, self-soothing, masochistic pleasure. The stuff of the death drive; the videogame logic of n deaths and n+1 lives. In a variety of ways, I see myself dying and dead in third person, camera drawing back, fading to black. Another technique I learned from my favourite entertainment. Amusing ourselves to death, death to amuse ourselves.

---

9   See
     https://www.brisbanetimes.com.au/national/queensland/brisba
     ne-airport-evacuated-20070414-ge8kew.html

(Something I never learned from the media: the psychic harm of repeated death dreams. Nobody told me not to fixate; maybe the adults were busy with their fantasies too.)

Eventually, my death-trance is broken. Turns out there is no threat. No bombs, guns or flaming planes. I never learn what caused the evacuation, and the violent men I imagined regress into the stillness of dreams. My sincere fear had become an absurdity. We return to the terminal, an arrival of the terrorised. Then we get on our planes and fly home. The holding pattern in the blue air.

On that day nothing happened. But hear the ambiguity: really, nothing did happen, because nothing nearly happened. The terror, the death-scare, the dread of nothing at all descended on me. I feared a future that could but did not come. I dragged a possible future into the present, a future where all anxiety would be relieved through destruction. Where terror brought an end to terror by drenching it in emptiness. The embrace of fear and imagination brought that impossible nothingness, death, into our world for a moment, only for it to slip back into inexistence an hour later. The collapse of the boundary between the false and true, the artifice and the real; the narrative structure of terror and entertainment, the nihilistic fiction.

Really, nothing happened that day because nothing nearly happened.

V
Natality

As I write this essay, I ask my mother if anything terrible happened when I was young. A trauma that explains it all.

She said 9/11.

This is a good answer. But I was a little surprised at her choice; I didn't know how she felt about the day, and I didn't know she was aware of my fear. Neither at the time nor afterwards had she really spoken about the event. She had said nothing.

At the time I didn't understand this consciously, but now I realise her silence was a signifier. Speechlessness is an act of speech: silence is a decision 'not-to,' a confession of 'unable-to.' For my mother and for me the unspeakable had happened and in her quiet she communicated nothing to me. In silence, death was born in our family home.

My mother, my siblings and I shared an experience of terror once; we never spoke about it. Fifteen years old this time. We are in a shopping mall at Christmas time. While we buy imported goods, management receives a phone call: someone has planted a bomb in the building. The loudspeakers tell us to leave in an orderly fashion. Anarchy naturally ensues. Unthinking, not-thinking, thinking of nothing, we race back to our car parked beneath the mall's glistening halls. But we aren't the only ones to run towards the underworld; there is a traffic jam in the carpark. We are stuck.

Among those cars, those bodies encased in metal, we realise we are trapped. If the bomb explodes and the building collapses, we are dead. In the car, unable to move, we sit silently. The ghosts of bombings past, seen only in the media, begin their spirit-play in the back of my mind.

I don't know if my mother is thinking of death or terror, but a resigned quiet fills the car. We hear the thrumming engine, the tinnitic whine, the thumping heart. We hear the murmurings of life's final frontier. We hear the sound of nothing. The car steadily moves, and then, sunshine; we are safe from another terror attack.

Later, we learn that this one was entirely imagined too. The artifice and the real: the bomb at the shopping centre was yet another fiction devised for the communication of terror.

VI
The Sublime

Today our lives are lived through media-events; the communication of terror is the limit experience of our world of images, while our world of images is built and revised through terror.

When terror screams out of nothingness it floods into the media, moving our vast communication apparatuses and endless crowds into motion, provoking a deluge of information and news articles, stories and secrets. A burst of language erupts after terror, redefining our world and changing the words we use. Like entertainment it gives us a new fiction we can confuse with the world.

The communication of terror changes things, cities, people. It leaves a blast residue: a strange combination of imperfect data and fearful dreams, distorted subjectivities and incomplete objectivity. Splinters of fiction mixed with fragments of truth. It intervenes in becoming, re-sculpting the self and re-channelling time; it produces a new narrative, born through the blood sacrifice of another story. Terror creates an obscure meaning whose nuance is only discovered through whispers and time; through words and history.

Terror, then, is a language event; an organising fiction, a deep narrative structure. It is a detonation of words that reorder the energies of the world. To borrow from Heidegger, [10] terror can be seen as a kind of linguistic technology that organises society and operates on men and machines alike.

Through media, terror becomes something like the idea of God or a forgotten trauma. After an attack, we who speak the language of terror assume formation. We begin to swing hypnotically between an unbearable chatter and a plangent stillness, genuflecting to the dread that suffuses our world. After we feel the terror of communication we consent to becoming terrorised; in fear and pleasure, we start to transform our world and ourselves with our new words.

---

[10] See *The Question Concerning Technology & Other Essays.*

VII
The Will to Knowledge

As an adult, 18 years old, there was a day when my death fantasies almost spilled into reality. I became the subject of a moment of unmediated terror, and a truth, murmuring in me since I was a boy, humming in my dreams, was revealed at a deafening volume. With a burst of words I found out who I had become. I saw how my subjectivity had been warped by the fiction of terror; how the artifice had changed the real.

It is March 8th, 2013; the city mall serves as the theatre of violence. I am inside a store with my girlfriend, immersed in my own thoughts. The terror begins without warning, like it arrived from outside the story, cracking the narrative of ordinary days.

Someone draws a gun outside the store, maybe ten metres down the mall, and violence erupts in the aureate glow of the department store. Amid the olfactory anarchy of perfume parlours the staff tell us to flee. Amazingly they remain; extending the logic of labour markets, they prepare to give their lives to their store.

Cortisol floods my blood and I turn to leave. I pace through the store, a blend of calm and cardiac cataclysm. The blood-thud, the Darwinian thrum, the feral bid to live. Haunted by fear's untimely ghosts, I expect the echoing crack of a revolver in the marmoreal hall, tiles shattering and blood smattering. In terror, in awe, some fool then screams what may or may not be fiction: 'He's coming.' (Incidentally this was correctly gendered.)

So maybe dreams do come true.

The crowd starts to sprint. Memories of stampede scenes; documentary footage of animals trampling the savannah. Visions for the exodus, for the transmigration of souls. I trot along, a frightened mammal, and I quickly reach the escalator. There I collide with a woman pushing a baby in a pram. We step backwards, I see her tiny child, and immediately we understand: we must decide who is first in line. Exodus. Terrified, we both know we are competing for scarcity; applied microeconomics at the mall. We lock eyes and collide again, both afraid to go last. I look at her baby, prelinguistic and strangely serene. I wonder what it sees in my eyes.

Time is running out. A roar of voices surrounds us. Language collapsing like blasted architecture, like sundered skyscrapers. In our animal panic, I then witness the eternal return of maternal instinct. She says, 'Get the fuck out of my way, you cunt.'

Great violence burns in her eyes; the murderous urges of women with children.

As a mother's child, I respect her sentiment.

I, the cunt, get the fuck out of her way.

She steps onto the escalator and I follow, an atmospheric clamour gathering around me. A sense of sound and fury and vision and violence. The gasps of nothing.

Though I willingly acquiesced to her command, I feel an ambivalence arise from deep within me. I realise I regret my decision, and I find I hate myself for my masochistic passivity. Then I surprise myself with a truth I had always known but hadn't yet thought. I realise I would have killed the mother and her child if it was necessary for my survival. I am certain I would destroy them both to escape the coming nothingness. Involuntarily, a strange, distant pleasure at the thought—in awe of the image.

Verity. When I ran from the gunman, I heard the loud, silent secret that had murmured in the back of my mind for a decade. Terror's death-scare, the fright of the abyss, had prepared me for selfish murder. I, the terrorised, was ready to commit terror; I had always been a hypocrite.

I get off the escalator and I run back to my hotel room, relentlessly speculating about planes and bombs and violent skies. I arrive at my room, storeys above the city streets, and from the window I see black police vans rushing towards the mall. Sirens soaked in reverb plash against the glass. Rigid with fear, I turn on the television and unlock my phone. I want to drown in the infinity of images; I need to write the fiction that will sustain my future death dreams.

The news of the siege unfolds before me, streaming forth from three sources: hand, wall, the air itself. Blackened by death dreams, sealed in an umbral cocoon, I surround myself with endless repetitions of the violence I had just escaped. The world into entertainment, entertainment into the world. In passive terror-pleasure, I re-terrorise myself because I need to know: was I safe? was death at bay? The will to knowledge: awaiting answers, I saturate myself in violent light. I turn up the brightness and the volume, hoping that pictures and sound can stop the trembling; a faith that images can inoculate me against death.

(Here, an involuntary memory, the brilliance of the unconscious: 'That's so cool!' my friend says.)

Bathing in the blue light, I think I am protecting myself. But really, I know I am merely abiding the anxious habit I learned years ago; I am adding another layer to the self built through the communication of terror. Belit by violent images, I encase myself in shadow: the accretion of a narcissistic heart.

VIII
The Categorical Imperative

Dread is an easy route to egotism. The bedrock shockwaves of terror, over a decade old, had written this truth upon my body; it left stress-fractures in my bones. This moment of fear revealed an individualism within me that would accept matricide and infanticide in exchange for a few more years of life. Adumbrated by the anxiety of nothingness, the terror of terror, my consciousness had been remodelled; a profound narcissism had colonised my heart.

Selfishness is the predictable result of a perpetual death-scare. Yet until I ran from this gunman my fear-borne egotism had remained unconscious. It prevailed in my previous encounters with terror—what is the focus on death-fantasies in a time of crisis but a form of narcissism, an inexcusable solipsism?—but my egotism had not fully revealed itself until that moment at the mall. Then, I found a brutal, awfully lonely ethic of self-preservation propelled by an archaic dread written upon my soul;

I found a language of death delivered by the communication of terror.

I had a discussion with my father once—a who-should-die-type ethical scenario. It involved a baby, a drug addict and a cancer researcher. My father chose to save the baby. He was adamant: you always save the child. My father had a clear moral law; we respect his firmness. I had always thought I was an ethical man like him; in a way, this is exactly what I learned that day. For after my encounter with the gunman I glimpsed the shadow of my father's Kantian rigidity within me. I finally read the universal law of individualism etched upon my heart: it simply said, 'the self before others.'

Those suicide-pilots of 9/11 had an effect far beyond their initial impact. Operating through the media of television, imagination and dreams, through language itself, they prepared me to behave with the disregard for life I so despised in the terrorists themselves. Their terror was not just a strike at the material world: it was the start of a war against the soul, waged to populate our world with people like themselves.

IX
Performativity

Violence reveals the most dreadful parts of our souls; it also creates them. Before the day I escaped this gunman my narcissism had lain hidden. But when my terror fantasies threatened to become reality, the awful truth fell into the light. Now it is clear. The death dreams of a modern soul; these are the provenance of its selfishness, its loneliness.

Ironically it seems the gunman committed his violence to escape his own isolation. As I learned from the news playing in my hotel room, after he drew his weapon, he pointed his gun at his own head. Then he threatened to send himself into the darkness. After he terrorised everyone in his vicinity, he screamed at the police. 'Shoot me,' he cried, cracked voice shattering through the mall.

The gunman was not murderous; he was suicidal.[11] And at the centre of his masochistic violence, we find a savage loneliness. When he started his act, he was grieving a friend who shot himself through the head during another police siege. He was also separated from his children, and his violence was a desperate bid to see them. We know this because he tried to phone his children while the police surrounded him; [12] we know this because the call failed, and he waved goodbye via CCTV instead.

There is a further involution. Despite the gunman's apparently suicidal intentions, his weapon was unloaded; he had no desire to hurt anyone. To all appearances it was real, yet his act was a performance of terror—a stage-play of self-annihilation, a pantomime violence. His was a simulated siege that erased the boundary between the false and the true, the artifice and the real: it was a meaninglessness with meaningful power.

So why did he (not) do it? For entertainment? For pleasure?

The playwright clarified his intentions: after his arrest, the gunman said his performance made him feel 'powerful'—like he 'was in control for once.'[13] To him, his act signified a resurgent will to power; he was railing against a chaotic life ravaged by drugs and violence. His death-play worked on two levels, then: at once, it explored the possibility of provoking his death; it also signified a desire for dominance *within* life. Striving for both destruction and control, the gunman gave his audience a contradictory set of symbols. The same actions simultaneously produced symbols of death and empowerment, making him, the

---

[11] Incidentally, I also found out that the gunman was arrested once more in 2018. This time he stabbed someone to death.

[12] See   https://www.abc.net.au/news/2018-07-13/queen-street-mall-gunman-wanted-over-stabbing-death/9990200

[13] See https://www.brisbanetimes.com.au/national/queensland/queen-street-mall-gunman-wants-to-work-with-atrisk-kids-20170801-gxnc0x.html

protagonist of his play, an ambivalent and indeterminate character. A sign of terror, a sign of pleasure.

The gunman's play was deeply ambiguous; ultimately, though, it led neither to death nor empowerment. Instead, it ended predictably: he was arrested and imprisoned. Deprived of his children and the chance to join his friend in death, his play left him nothing but the brutal isolation of the penal system. The gunman's ambitions were thwarted. Yet we should not read his imprisonment as a failure, but a partial synthesis of his themes. Had the gunman attained death or authority he would have placed himself beyond life or above society: he would have gained total isolation or become a successful self-made individual. While these ideals did not manifest in our world, through imprisonment he gained what is common to both death and empowerment: lonely individuality.

With an unloaded gun one man started a theatre of terror. He, the artist, created a real fiction of death; we, the victims, consumed his art when his actions were broadcast into our homes. When he drew his gun, his death-scare was immediately translated into dead images. Because of our society's appetite for terror, spectacle and the language of death—in short, our demand for trauma, for painful entertainment, for terror and awe, all at once—the dread he caused was multiplied. Through the mass-media, his violence was amplified and immortalised: we chose to make it unforgettable and allowed ourselves to become isolated and terrorised in its light. Not only did his violence act as a symbol of individualism, then: it also showed how the media's images of terror cultivate the individual's violent indifference, how we both want and fear our visions of death.

The gunman united the medium and his message. Like 9/11, the gunman's performance was therefore a piece of nihilistic theatrical genius. With his literary act—'literary' because his actions really did nothing except rewrite consciousnesses, author news broadcasts, and add to our shared fiction of terror—he confirmed the symbolic equivalence of loneliness, individualism and death by using a meaningless gesture. There was no truth to his violence, yet his acts had a traumatic effect on the consciousness of the world: his theatre was translated into images that joined the deluge of dread flowing from our screens, the flood that terrorises us into individualistic self-enclosure. Amplified through our mass media apparatus, his faux-siege became a particularly modern event; it was the mirror-image of a PR conference, a forerunner of fake news, for once it was depicted it didn't matter if it was true or false: it meant nothing but still it managed to inflame our fear of death, our terror of nothingness.

Built upon layers of loneliness the gunman's act was a pure embodiment of nihilism: it gave us a sign of nothing, a symbol of death all the more radical for its total untruth. As we know, the symbol of death is the very basis of trauma; it is also the lifeblood of media. True or not, the violent sign contains a meaning that sustains our culture: we thrive on its implied nothingness. Perhaps this is because of its emptiness. With these images, weightless even when they are true, we can repeat the violence until we are traumatised into numbness. With fear-laden language we can create the meaningful meaninglessness we depend on; we can sleep and die with our familiar death-dreams. All our culture needs is the communication of terror, true or false; with it, we can secure our deep narrative structures—our individualistic fiction, our loneliness, our terror of communication.

X
The Terror of Communication

How did the gunman's siege end? I can't confirm it, but I believe the police shot him. In his siege the gunman sought death; the police nearly obliged his demands.[14] An article tells us it was only

---

[14]   A real-time news report of the event tells us the police used rubber bullets to subdue the gunman; later that day, the police

by the police officers' professionalism that he lived—that they didn't kill him with the deadly bullets they fired into his body.[15] (How far that humble little word has come—professionalism! It is far afield from its home in the church, the law and medicine.)

With his moment of terror, the gunman gained a near-death experience and a penal conviction. Though his crime was born of loneliness and desperation, he ironically confirmed and deepened his isolation. His story is a tragedy: he tried to escape his loneliness and reaffirmed it through his acts. It was also a particularly modern violence in that it united the aggressor and his city in individualism, binding us all together beneath a profound loneliness. Because his play inspired a fervent drive for self-protection in us, we learned we were as violently individualistic as he; that we, individuals of this city, were prepared to treat each other as objects in our bid to live; that we were isolated like the gunman.

On the day of the gunman's play I experienced a simulation of the terror I have feared since 9/11. Terror has now entered my life directly and through the media; while the real was artifice and the mediated was true, I now see the similarities between direct perception and image. To me, mediated terror is not categorically different to the direct perception of violence: rather, the difference lies in the severity of their effects. Whether it occurs in person or through a screen, terrorism inflames the

---

said the man was 'not shot with a gun.' But elsewhere in the same article, a witness report says that the siege ended with the gunman 'lying on the ground "covered in blood".' And both a personal connection privy to the police operation and a profile of the gunman released four years later concerning an unconnected murder, tell us that he was hit with '[l]ethal and non-lethal rounds' when the police opened fire on him.

[15]　See https://www.brisbanetimes.com.au/national/queensland/queen-street-mall-gunman-wants-to-work-with-atrisk-kids-20170801-gxnc0x.html and https://www.abc.net.au/news/2013-03-08/gunman-in-brisbane27s-queen-street-mall/4560712

fear of death and heightens the drive to self-preservation. It amplifies our fear and sends us into crazed, defensive egotism; it strengthens our desire for violent self-enclosure and protection against otherness. In other words, terror drives individualism and loneliness to their apogee: murder, suicide, death, blackness.

The terrorist is a mirror image of the individualist, for they both aim at narcissistic isolation. Terror is a narcissistic act that encourages narcissism in its victims.[16] Ironically, terror produces a second kind of terror. It produces the kind of terrifying loneliness that can lead someone to think of murdering a mother and child to protect themselves; where a man would hold a gun to his head, threatening suicide so he could see his kids; where a child can see images of death and scream his approval without thought for whether it is entertainment or terror.

(Narcissistic isolation, the terror of communication, the lack of care for others; once again, the collapse of the boundary between the artifice and the real.)

At the bleak extreme of terrorism, all aims towards death, loneliness, individualism. Yet at this limit, we can finally see what lies beyond terror. Though we may not hear it yet, there is a glimmer of hope in the gunman's violence; this comes from the fact that his terror was a communicative act. When our gunman drew his weapon the cameras were already aimed at him; it was only a matter of time until images cascaded outwards into the world, multiplied into infinity as they spread through the internet and our minds, where his play would be preserved as data or bent memories of dread and trauma. Its passage into media, into a terror of images, was inevitable; this we have known since men tore the sky apart in September 2001. Though he failed in his bid for connection, his violence nonetheless implies a desperate need for human relationships. The consequences of his actions, nothing less than a Mass Media Event, render this

---

[16] Paradoxically, the dynamic between terror and individualism ends with a collective demand for self-enclosure against the threat of otherness; that is, individualism ends in fascism.

indisputable. He spoke and we listened: communication, albeit of a terrible kind, was established.

'Communication' comes from the Latin '*communicare*,' a word that literally means 'to make common.' In our world of mass media his and all other acts of terror can only be communicative acts—no matter their meaning, they always express something that is made common. But as a communicative act, terror contradicts itself. Terror must be made common to push us towards isolation. To produce narcissistic self-enclosure in its victims, it necessarily assumes a responsive audience. Even if it aims at individualism, terror speaks first of our community, our human relations, of the language we share with others. Terror should not only remind us of the nihilistic death, our individual isolation, or the masochistic entertainments of anxiety; it should more fundamentally remind us of their opposites; life, community, and our shared languages where communication is possible.

Communicating with violence refracted into a million images is not the only way to speak; nor is violence the sole purpose of communication. It must be asked: why would someone reveal their inner self in such a clamorous way? Of all possible language games, why terror? I cannot say for sure. But a resounding violence only becomes a need, I suspect, when you believe that your voice has become as quiet as death. Violence is the passion of those that must urgently express themselves to a world that has become deaf to their cries. The individual, traumatised by past violence, emits a boundless scream into an infinite silence. Where their life has become so lonely that they might as well be dead, they abandon everything and commit an act that the world must hear. Had the gunman's inner world been seen and heard earlier—or, perhaps, had he not been subjected to the kind of violence that leads you to shout—he may not have fallen into the silence where terrible fantasies fester, where visions of bullets and planes ripping, screaming through the air reach an infinite volume.

Only the desperate and quiet truly need the volume of the world's media. Terror is the loud language of death; addressed in this tongue, we are always free to respond in kind. But we can also reply with something else. Affronted with violence, we should find the words we need to communicate a different language; to speak not with a language of death, but of life.

XI
Nihilism

A final memory. I could stop now, but there's nothing to speak of.

I am 23 years old. June, 2017. Florence, Italy. A Radiohead concert, with support from James Blake and Junun. I'm there alone.

Context: the communication of terror reached new heights in this year. In May an Islamic extremist, aged 22, just too young to be my twin, bombed Ariana Grande's concert in Manchester, murdering 22 people, including some children.[17] Days before, while I was in Paris, a Syrian man attempted a terror attack at the Notre Dame cathedral; police shot him in the chest.[18] Earlier in the year, ISIS declared their intention to attack Italy: 'We will conquer your Rome, break your crosses, and enslave your women', they said; meanwhile, Radiohead angered people worldwide by announcing a concert in Israel.[19]

The logical implication, the irrational belief: ISIS will bomb the Radiohead concert.

---

[17] See
https://www.nytimes.com/2017/05/22/world/europe/ariana-grande-manchester-police.html
[18] See https://www.bbc.com/news/world-europe-40178183
[19] See
https://www.theatlantic.com/magazine/archive/2015/03/what-isis-really-wants/384980/ and
https://www.rollingstone.com/music/music-news/thom-yorke-breaks-silence-on-israel-controversy-126675/

My anxiety is severe when I go to the concert. I try to enjoy it. But I spend the whole time screaming at myself: I am certain there will be an attack; I am also certain that I am wrong. Given the clamour within, my world is overwritten by this terrified dispute.

'Phew, for a minute there / I lost myself', Thom Yorke sings at one point. A rush of serotonin. Blood to the head. I burn with anxiety and pleasure; I reach the limits of entertainment, terror and awe, all at once. On the brink of the sublime, the *ekstasis* of being, fantasies at the brink of imaginary death. Rushes of pleasure and fear.

'I'm not here / This isn't happening', he sings on a track that plays in my mind, a track they don't perform. Raging with words of terror, my mind dissociates from my body, silencing the music seeping into my nerves. Strobe lights and blown speakers; I am deaf and blind. I ask someone to take pictures of me, I think of suicide, I post them online. Images bleed out of the event. Communication and terror. The world into entertainment, entertainment into the world. Days later I remember nothing of the event; years later, I write about the nothing at the event.

At the concert, the evening's reality is swallowed beneath my false expectation of fear. All night, music combats the language of death; their conflict thunders loudly, silently over everything else. And this time, standing at the limit of terror, next to nothing, I can truly say: nothing happened, I was entertained.

My training in the language of death, I think, was completed that night; like a terrorist, I could now make nothing out of something and negate the world with dreams of death. The holding pattern in the blue air; the erasure of the boundary between the false and the true, the artifice and the real.

Do Nothing! An Alternative to Birth-Strikes

BIRTH-STRIKERS [1] ARE A GROUP OF PEOPLE who believe it is immoral to have children because children contribute to climate change and climate change is going to fuck the planet.[2] The birth-strikers have started a procreative rebellion; they refuse to reproduce until the climate crisis is averted.

Though they have been around for a while, you have probably heard about the birth-strikers in recent months; left-leaning publications like *The Guardian* love this shit. Extinction Rebellion dumped 200 litres of artificial blood on the ground outside 10 Downing Street to symbolise the 'death of our children' from climate change; some of them did so as part of the birth-strike movement.[3] An activist named Blythe Pepino has

---

[1]   By this, I don't mean the formal group, BirthStrike, founded in 2018. I mean people who agree with the sentiments expressed below, who I have been aware of since 2016. According to Google's Ngram viewer, usage of the term dates to before World War I. Birth-strikes, it seems, have occurred for different reasons throughout history.

[2]   Note that these are not the same group as the antinatalists, which encompasses philosophers who argue against the continuation of human life, and whose ridiculous position is secured by sham metaphysics and hidden assumptions.

[3]   See
https://www.theguardian.com/lifeandstyle/2019/mar/12/birthst

started a protest group, 'BirthStrike,' to promote the movement, and her efforts scored her an interview with Fox News' Tucker Carlson. [4] Progressive darling Alexandria Ocasio-Cortez also endorsed the birth-strike logic in an Instagram livestream: 'It is basically a scientific consensus that the lives of our children are going to be very difficult,' she said, 'and it does lead young people to have a legitimate question: is it okay to still have children?'[5] We don't know if Ocasio-Cortez is a birth-striker herself; nonetheless, her thinking is shared by millennials who are terrified of life on a sweltering planet, and so refuse to bring children into our world.

At heart, the birth-striker attempts a logical, moral argument. A 40-year-old mother, quoted in *The Guardian* on November 27th, succinctly captures their motivations: 'I regret having my kids because I am terrified that they will be facing the end of the world due to climate change.'[6] Essentially, the birth-striker worries that child-rearing will a) accelerate and worsen climate change, and that b) the worsened climate change will inflict possibly unendurable suffering upon their offspring. Procreation, in their eyes, will contribute to the impending environmental disaster, and the children they create will be the ones who suffer most. Their brief lives will be snuffed out, or failing this they will be wholly occupied by existential anguish we can scarcely imagine. Theirs will be a world of 'wars over limited resources, collapsing civilisation, failing agriculture, rising seas, melting glaciers, starvation, droughts, floods, mudslides and widespread

---

rikers-meet-the-women-who-refuse-to-have-children-until-climate-change-ends

[4] See https://youtu.be/acuvOjf71gc

[5] See
https://www.theguardian.com/environment/shortcuts/2019/feb/27/is-alexandria-ocasio-cortez-right-to-ask-if-the-climate-means-we-should-have-fewer-children

[6] See
https://www.theguardian.com/environment/2020/nov/27/climate-apocalypse-fears-stopping-people-having-children-study

devastation,' to quote one anxious birth-striker, again from *The Guardian.* [7]

In essence the birth-striker believes our children will not have the lives we have had. They think the inter-generational drop in the quality of life due to climate change will be catastrophic, and the more we breed the worse it will be. Hence, they say, it is our duty not to bring life into the world. The moral dilemma is clear: to breed, or not to breed? A cogent thought, yet I wonder if there isn't a less suicidal solution to our environmental problems.

My questioning comes because, in my eyes, these catastrophe ethics are ethically catastrophic. Nietzsche proclaimed as nihilistic all moralities that constrained the will to power; to live, flourishing wildly, thriving at the highest tenor. Birth-striking is an obviously nihilistic approach to the climate crisis. Abstaining from procreation is life-denying in the most literal sense. [8] To use Pepino's words, the birth-strike offers genetic and species suicide as an antidote to the problem of unregulated industry and unsustainable capitalism. By birth-striking, individuals subordinate their biology to a crisis of political economy and consumption culture. A sense of powerlessness lies at its core, and it is, I think, a stance utterly devoid of hope. It contains a despair, forced upon the weak by those who are both powerful and indifferent. [9]

---

[7]   See
     https://www.theguardian.com/environment/2020/nov/27/clima
     te-apocalypse-fears-stopping-people-having-children-study

[8]   A caveat. Obviously, choosing not to have children if you don't want to have children is not nihilistic. The important thing is to affirm your desires. If you don't want children, and then have them for moral reasons, you could argue that this is closer to nihilism than abstaining. My argument is directed towards those who want to have children and procreate but deny themselves their literally life-affirming desires.

[9]   A counterpoint: bringing life into the world only for it to die horribly could also be construed as life-denying. Perhaps

Aside from its nihilism, [10] birth-striking individualises the solution to the climate crisis. We have been unable to hold our governments and multi-national corporations to account for their carbon emissions so far. And despite our talents for innovation, technological solutions to the crisis have not come quickly enough. Both, I think, are failures of capitalism: of money, continuously funnelled into the wrong locations. Whatever the case, people are disturbed by the disjunction between scientific consensus and political action; they feel this gap places the responsibility for species survival in their hands. Terrified, they take the most extreme action they can: vasectomies and tubal ligations to fight climate change. To preserve the species, they propose to wipe out the evolutionary line that stretches backwards from them to the first stirrings of life on earth. The seriousness and the tragedy of their protest, I think, can't be overstated. But neither can the inequity of their solution: to destroy your bloodline for the irresponsibilities of governments and corporations is manifestly unfair. Those who lose share little to none of the blame: the individual is, at best, a marginal contributor to climate change, and the unborn certainly did not cause the problem. [11]

My qualm is not with the logic of birth striking; indeed, I sympathise with it. I simply abhor the willingness of people to

---

breeding itself in the current context is nihilistic—another reason to protest climate change.

[10] And the patent irrationality of the position that implicitly insists that a life of suffering is worse than no life at all, despite the fact that we don't know what not-living is like, and therefore can't compare it to life.

[11] Christine Overall, quoted in Elizabeth Kolbert's *New Yorker* article, 'The Case Against Kids,' apparently believes that 'non-existent people have no moral standing.' I must disagree. With Derrida, I feel a responsibility for all other others—including those yet to come. To suggest otherwise imposes a limitation on our responsibility, even though our actions directly affect these potential people, and I don't see how you could justify doing so.

adopt this mantle of responsibility. Their choice shocks me in the way all political suicides do. Self-immolations against oppression, blowing your brains out for freedom and the like. They feel like non-violent protests gone wrong. And I wonder if there isn't another equilibrium—something more just than self-destruction.

In this mind I offer my solution: have your child, and shoot a banker instead. If overpopulation and overconsumption are our problems, reproduce and gun down a fossil fuels executive. Set the scales straight: kill a politician for each kid you have. Bomb the conference for oil industry lobbyists and start your family. For if you see a slow species suicide as your responsibility, why not murder instead? Balance can be achieved in different ways. To birth-strike, I think, only punishes ourselves, and deprives the unborn of their chance to live. Why not deprive those responsible of life instead?

Those in power are already sacrificing the next generation with their inaction: birth-striking obliges their logic. Instead, why not turn the tables on them? Why don't we sacrifice those in power to protect the most vulnerable, those most deprived of a political voice—our living children and the potential people yet to come? For the sake of their interests the powerful would love it if we ceased breeding; it suits them perfectly if we declare it immoral. Our morality would wipe out their competition and liberate them from their responsibility. Participating in the birth-strike, we inadvertently serve our leaders' selfish indifference and their entitlement. And what, I ask, is more immoral than forsaking the innocent to protect the powerful? In my eyes, the only greater crime is to make the mistake that the powerful will care that you abstained. The birth-strikers relieve them of their responsibility; they will be overjoyed at your generosity. You will have fulfilled their unstated hope for your death.

Eco-terrorism, then, really is more life-affirming than the birth-strike. If birth-strikes are permitted, then we should have more eco-terrorism. No?

Psychological arguments further support our case. Psychoanalytic theory, for example, tells us that suicide is often murder in a masochistic guise. Suicide kills the part of the other that lies within our hearts: as Sloterdijk writes, 'there are suicides who are basically murders of someone else.'[12] If our aggression really is towards the other, why not get our target right and take them down instead?

Lastly, certain humanist philosophers also conclude in our favour. As Albert Camus argued in *The Rebel*, once life is recognised as a good for one man, then it becomes one for all. Inversely, if suicide is enabled then so is murder. These violences are equivalent. Morally speaking, then, the birth strikers are not better than the businessman who callously destroys our environment: they answer the species suicide of climate change with the species suicide of the birth-strike. Political violence, on the other hand, would lay the responsibility for climate change in the right place. In this way, shooting a banker would be more just than the birth-strike. At the very least I suspect it would be more effective.

Now, I digress: the above was entirely ironic. In truth I believe that both murder and suicide are entirely immoderate positions. I deplore each of them equally. While they may appear more radical than inaction, neither option directly addresses the cause of the crisis. I also have severe doubts as to their pragmatic powers. And most importantly, having children is a profoundly hopeful act; the responsibility it entails only encourages our demand for climate action.

Rather than birth-strike, I ask you to be constructive with your blues: use your aggressive energies to hold those in power to account. Nothing will stop the relentless engines of industry and consumption except firm, proper accountability, enforced by the masses. We must aim towards a genuine responsibility enforced by the public in our political economy. I believe our goal is not so far away as we might think. If the birth-striker has both the power and abilities of abstract reasoning sufficient to wipe out their evolutionary line, then surely they can muster the energy to protect our planet in a more meaningful way.

---

[12]   *Critique of Cynical Reason*, p.91.

I conclude, then, by reminding the reader that atrocities occur only with the consent of the masses. Slavoj Žižek once wrote that doing absolutely nothing is the most violent and effective way to protest our capitalist system;[13] our economy survives only as long as we participate in a frenzied cycle of production and consumption, a debt-fuelled cycle whose closure is infinitely deferred by necessity. With this kind of violently non-violent inaction in mind, we must all withdraw our consent to the 'species suicide'[14] of climate change, to our political economy where catastrophe appears inevitable for absurd reasons, and to our world where ridiculous thought experiments of the birth-striking kind have any value whatsoever. Only then, I believe, can we feel optimistic about a world where human life exists.

---

[13]   *Violence*, p.183.
[14]   The words are Blythe Pepino's, from her interview with Fox News' Tucker Carlson. See https://youtu.be/acuvOjf71gc

Work & Mourning:
A Theory of Depression

'And, when our lives crack, and the loveliest mirror cracks, is it not right to rest, to step aside and heal?'
—Sylvia Plath, writing in her journal

'God is imagined as saying: "Illness was no doubt the final cause of the whole urge to create. By creating, I could recover; by creating, I became healthy."'
—Heinrich Heine on the Creation,
quoted in Freud's *On Narcissism: An Introduction*

I
The Morning of Work

ON THE MORNING OF WORK, my father heard his mother had died in the night. A phone call to his office brought the news: at 10am he learned she succumbed to cancer in her sleep. My father thanked the caller and hung up the phone. It was a Wednesday.

My father, a doctor, was a cardiologist. He worked with the heart. The human heart. He had an important job that saved lives, and that morning he had a full day of consultations ahead of him. I don't know how he felt when he received the call. I don't know if he knew either. But I know he decided it was too late to cancel his appointments. My father, a doctor, was a cardiologist. He worked with the heart. The human heart. So, in the wake of the deathly news he worked all day.

My father came home at 6pm. He stood at the end of the kitchen bench. Eyes averted, he told us what had happened. His mother had stopped her cancer treatments; they made her feel life was not worth living so she ended chemotherapy and embraced her end. I, a fourteen-year-old, said I understood. My father said that I didn't understand. Then we were silent. Eventually he left for his study to arrange the funeral.

Two days later we flew 2000 kilometres to attend the wake. We stayed two nights in my father's hometown. He had not lived there for 24 years, but he visited once a year during his annual leave. The funeral was on a Saturday. His sister, his only remaining relative aside from his children and wife, attended the funeral with her own kids. My father was sad, but I didn't see him cry. Apparently he wept privately. I was also sad, but I didn't cry. I did not weep privately.

On Sunday we flew 2000 kilometres back to my hometown. My father's worktown. On Monday, he returned to work. And then he kept working. And working. And working. At dawn he'd rise for work not to mourn and we would stay silent about her death. The time had passed for the work of mourning.

If I had to guess, it was after his mother's funeral that my father became angry. Closed. Where his depression, still ever-present after twelve years, took root in the heart of our family. But who can say, really?

Over the years my father's sad fury deepened; adjacent to his despair I learned that death resists our understanding. Death. We don't know what it means. We don't even know if it can't be understood. Dead. His mother was dead and what could he say about it? Death. This is what ignorance feels like. My grandmother was dead and what could I say about what we should say about it? Dead. Can we say if life should be saved or death embraced? Or if he had done the right thing? Nothing. Nothing? Should we talk about it forever or say nothing of it at all? Dead. What does that word even mean?

Today, I sometimes think my father was right to be quiet. To rush headlong into work, to bury his grief beneath time made full by duty. To pitch into the past what he had lost forevermore and become silent with his love. But I also wonder if questioning was necessary. If, for the dead, we should endure an uncertain time of unfolding ambiguity, of echoing why, of mournful music. Whether we should respect the end through a threnody of questioning, where the voice is a counterpoint to the blinding quiet.

Perhaps. But who can say anything about the truth of dying and the work of mourning? Neither him, nor me, nor her. Time passes, in any case and in speech or silence, life steps out of the dark while death strides into the light. The bright-work and shadow-play of being. How we see anything at all. The broken home of love.

II
The Work of Mourning

Loss, work and depression; today, we practise a strange mourning ritual that binds them together. It goes like this. Each day, people like my father lose the ones they love; afterwards, they immure themselves in their work; and as their lives unfold in the absence of their love they descend into depression's dark well. Bereaved, busy and miserable: this daylit constellation of symptoms benights homes and offices everywhere. Often it is ignored and sometimes it is encouraged; most commonly there is a tacit acceptance of its logic. Beneath our acquiescence to this contemporary mourning ritual, however, lies an attitude of neglect. Few of us can say why loss, work and depression are linked; fewer still can say whether this is a good, healthy thing or whether we ought to mourn our losses in another way.

For the sake of ourselves, our loved ones and perhaps for death itself, we must interrogate this practice that we unthinkingly abide. Loss, work and depression: we must see what draws them together. We begin by examining the link between grief, mourning and depression; then we examine the role of work in this ritual.

In recent years, the illness known as 'depression' has reached epidemic proportions in the United States. A 2020 report by their National Center for Health Statistics tells us that in 2018 an 'estimated 7.2% of American adults had a major depressive episode in the past year,' while between 2015–18 13.2% of adults had used antidepressants in the thirty days preceding the survey. We also learn that antidepressant usage rises with age: people aged 60 and over, who are most likely to have lost loved ones and are probably closest to death, use antidepressants at more than twice the rate of young people.[1]

America, it seems, is rather depressed. But what this means for the society and its people, its healthcare system and indeed for the nation's soul is not entirely clear. It is hard to say how much of its depression America could realistically eliminate; inversely we are even less able to say how much depression America must tolerate. Complicating matters, this disclarity is linguistic as much as it is medical. 'Depression,' we read, is a 'common destination to which many pathways lead': it is a symptom with a wide variety of sources that can emerge from a combination of 'one or any several of these pathways.'[2] The word 'depression' is a catch-all term for a set of physical and psychological symptoms with a complex, varied aetiology that encompasses biological, social, spiritual and mental factors. There is not one 'depression' but many different 'depressions' and to treat these depressions properly we must employ a context-appropriate strategy that accounts for all the relevant aspects of the patient's life.

Among all these depressions, of particular interest to us is the one formerly known as 'melancholia' among psychoanalysts. A forerunner to our contemporary category of 'depression,' in many ways melancholia is indistinguishable from other forms of depression. It too involves a lack of energy, low self-esteem, anhedonia and a habit of self-reproach. But unlike biochemical

---

[1]   See https://www.cdc.gov/nchs/products/databriefs/db377.htm

[2]   *The Noonday Demon*, p.302.

depressions, which ostensibly manifest due to imbalances or deficiencies in the brain of serotonin, dopamine and norepinephrine, melancholia has its roots in a fundamental and painful psychological phenomenon: loss and the 'work of mourning' it provokes.[3]

'The work of mourning' is a phrase first introduced by Freud in his essay, 'Mourning & Melancholia,' a work where he tried to establish a link between mourning and melancholic depression, which he believed shared some symptoms. His theory is complex, but we can understand its most important aspects by his use of the word 'work.' For Freud, mourning really is a kind of work: it is an arduous psychological process that allows us to overcome the grief born when we lose someone or something we love. This process has a specific purpose for our psyches—it produces a new symbolic understanding of the world that remains after we have lost something significant, allowing us to overcome our grief—and it requires our energy, time, and attention if we are to complete it. Much like the concept of 'work' in physics, which is defined as the product of force and physical displacement, mourning consumes our energy to displace our grief; Freud rightly calls this process the 'work' of mourning.

Psychoanalyst Darian Leader's excellent study of depression, *The New Black*, further illuminates the work of mourning. Following Freud, Leader believes mourning is a strangely creative symbolic work. Unlike the loss that subtracts our beloved from the world, mourning is a positive act carried out by the psyche that produces a new understanding of the world that

---

[3] Even Freud distinguishes melancholia from other types of depression. In 'Mourning and Melancholia,' he writes: 'Melancholia… appears in various different clinical forms; these do not seem amenable to being grouped together into a single entity, and some of them suggest somatic rather than psychogenetic diseases.'

acknowledges our beloved's absence.[4] Though it concerns loss, Leader says this act is necessarily creative: our memories, hopes and ideas of our loved one are not automatically transformed when we lose them, so our minds have to produce new words and symbols to register our loss on the psychic level. In a way, mourning involves the production of a new language of loss; it demands that we use our words to judge our world, eliminate the dead from our desires and dreams, and rebuild ourselves around the fact that our love is gone. Mourning gives us a grief poetry we can use to express our loss.

Mourning is time-consuming, draining and utterly painful. Yet this work is necessary if we want to live in a home where the dead have been put to rest. Without mourning, we will be haunted forevermore by someone who is lost but not gone; they will survive as a symbol in our minds and false hopes will litter our dreams. Mourning is essential; yet as with other kinds of work the bereaved can either succeed or fail when they begin the process. Mourning can be frustrated, and if this frustration is extreme enough, we can develop the psychopathology known as 'melancholia.'

Like mourning, melancholia is a kind of language. If the former helps us define absence, then the latter is its obverse: melancholia is a creative act or judgment that says the work of mourning can't proceed, that denies the symbolic truth of our loss. Not all frustrated mourning becomes melancholia:[5] we tend

---

[4] Leader says mourning proceeds in four stages, and designates these as: 'framing the loss,' 'killing the dead,' removing the lost love from our desires and redefining the self. These aren't directly important to our discussion here; we only need to know that each step is a different positive and creative symbolic act.

[5] As Leader writes, 'a blocked, interrupted or failed mourning is not the same thing as melancholia.' (p.168). Most acts of mourning are frustrated in some way—who could unfailingly give the work the energy it needs every moment, especially if their grief lasts for months or years?—and it is only in specific circumstances that mourning becomes melancholia.

to speak this language when some aspect of our loss or its related emotions are unconscious[6] or repressed.[7] There are many factors that can lead us to repress a loss; among the most important, however, is our degree of identification with the lost object. When we identify too powerfully with our beloved, their absence can compromise our self-integrity; if we lose them forever, it can be an existentially threatening experience.[8] A strong level of identification can also leave us feeling ambivalent towards our beloved object, binding us to them through a powerful mixture of love and hate. Such ambivalence may prevent us consciously admitting our feelings and processing our loss; doing so would produce an inadmissible level of guilt.

---

[6] Ibid; 'Mourning and Melancholia' in *The Future of an Illusion*, p.76.

[7] Sylvia Plath's novel *The Bell Jar* presents an example of a character whose mourning is repressed. Esther Greenwood's father died when she was young, and her mother never allowed the family to mourn his absence: 'I thought it odd that in all the time my father had been buried in this graveyard, none of us had ever visited him,' Esther says at one point. 'My mother hadn't let us come to his funeral because we were only children then, and he had died in hospital, so the graveyard and even his death, had always seemed unreal to me. I had a great yearning, lately, to pay my father back for all the years of neglect... and it seemed fitting I should take on a mourning my mother had never bothered with.... I remembered that I had never cried for my father's death. My mother hadn't cried either.' (p.161) After Esther sinks into melancholy as a young adult, her recovery depends on her a) expressing her grief for her lost father, and b) expressing her hatred towards her mother (p.195) which was partly caused by the repression of this loss.

[8] Note that it is the strength of the identification, not the identification itself that is the issue. As Leader says on p.49, identification with the lost loved one 'is present to some extent in every mourning process,' as identification is part of every human relationship.

In relationships characterised by powerful identification, losing our loved one can be psychologically intolerable; if so, our psychological integrity may rely on us maintaining our identification in spite of the loss. This means we may have to symbolically 'die' alongside our beloved. Enacting our symbolic death, we enter a kind of death-in-life and immure ourselves in grief; we adopt a twilit mood and embrace the stillness of the abyss. Barely able to speak, in our velleity we transmute every moment of our lives into a single judgement: the melancholic denial of loss. Melancholia, then, is a refusal of reality. It is the depression of insurmountable absence; of grief gone awry; of lives made incomprehensible through loss. It is death's depression, a sadness of impossible love. It is the depression of men who lose their mothers; of parents whose children leave home forever; of young people displaced from places to which they cannot return.

To reiterate, not all depressions are melancholic episodes. But if Freud and Leader's theories are correct then the more psychoanalytically-minded should view the rising rate of depression around the world with great interest. A host of factors have undoubtedly contributed to the proliferation of this debilitating illness; among these we must entertain the possibility that our ability to mourn has been blocked. That somehow we are more likely to be frustrated in our attempts to process our losses.

The demands incumbent on the creative work of mourning may give us some insight into this frustration. Whether it is a piece of art or a human loss, a creative work demands much from its creator; like art, the work of mourning requires our care and attention. Freud knew this, and he wrote that mourning 'cannot be accomplished immediately... [it is] carried out piecemeal at great expenditure of time and investment of energy.'[9] Beyond these cognitive resources the creator must also try and permit the work a full degree of freedom. Whatever their fears and anxieties the work must unfold without constraints, achieving its natural tenor and final form free from interference or inhibition.

---

[9]   'Mourning and Melancholia' in *The Future of an Illusion*, p.75.

For mourning to proceed effectively the aggrieved must possess an artist's generosity of spirit. They must give the creative work of mourning the energy and freedom it requires. They must spend whatever time they need creating a language, a vocabulary, a judgement, a knowledge that adequately captures their loss. Yet sufficient acquiescence to the work is not always possible: many artworks and many losses are frustrated and remain incomplete. For artworks the consequences of this frustration are not clear— what can we say about the meaning of an aborted painting, an unfinished symphony?—but where the creative work of mourning is blocked or frustrated the consequences can be disastrous; it can lead to melancholia.

In this light we must consider our commitment to work. Work is a primary structuring force for adult life in most societies and the question of work sits at the heart of the modern conscience. More than almost anything else it consumes our time, energy, and freedom. And so work collides with melancholia; it competes for the same resources. In competition, work can aid or inhibit the creative work of mourning; as it demands sacrifices of us, it can also provoke the need to mourn. Work is deeply connected to the work of mourning, producing and frustrating it; to understand depression today, then, we must understand how labour and grief interact.

III
Working in Business

The morning of work and the work of mourning; faced with their competition, my father chose the former. He is not alone in this regard. Thousands of us made this choice today; thousands more will make it tomorrow. Silent and aggrieved we carry on. Noble, but I can't help noting how alone this leaves us: quietly labouring each day, adumbrated by a shadow of loss that falls beyond the narrow words we allow ourselves to say. Speechless and full of thought. Empty words and hurting hearts.

I don't know where my father learned this ethic, but I was taught it by my university.

During my undergraduate degree I suffered the indignity[10] of a course called Working in Business. As its name suggests the course taught us how to Work in Business. A fascinating curriculum: we learned about synergy, networks, conflict resolution. How to dress well; the firm handshake.[11] The ethics, the language, the ways of Being-in-the-world needed to Work in Business.

In this course they had the temerity to teach us about empathy. A multiple-choice quiz administered by our tutor assessed our Emotional Intelligence, a.k.a. 'EQ.' This was important: to Work in Business you need good EQ. That's a fact. Data supports it. Imagine networking with a low EQ: ridiculous. So don't complain. Just ensure you have a strong EQ. Otherwise? You're fucked. You cannot Work in Business.

Despite my sincere efforts I underperformed on the EQ quiz. I couldn't think like a man who wanted to Work in Business. My EQ was not good enough. What despair for my life, what shame. I mourned my lost future; I wept for the time, the Work, the Business, that became impossible.

Of the questions I answered wrongly on this quiz I remember one particularly well. 'You experience a loss in your personal life (a breakup of a relationship, a loss in your family, etc.),' it read. 'What is the best way to deal with the loss?'

There were four answers. Two of these ('C: Drink yourself into a stupor'; 'D: All of the above') were obviously wrong (D being incorrect because C was ridiculous), which left two feasible choices: 'A: Throw yourself into your work' and 'B: Take as much time as you need off work to process the loss.'

---

[10] Admittedly, partly self-inflicted.

[11] This is actually true. One of our assignments—an oral presentation—assessed us on our outfits and mannerisms, both of which needed to be 'context appropriate.'

I thought of my father when he lost his mother.

Ever an antagonistic child, I chose B.

The tutor marked the quiz; I got the wrong answer. The correct choice was 'A: Throw yourself into work.' I made a mistake because I believed emotions were more important than productivity. Incorrect. It would seem that such beliefs are a sign of deficient EQ. Low emotional intelligence. A lack of empathy. Clearly, I was not ready to Work in Business. I don't know if I ever will be.

IV
Inhibiting Mourning: The Production of (In)Difference

My university course positioned work as a panacea for grief. The work of mourning, it said, was best completed during the morning of work. The creative work of loss, where we fashion our judgment and declare our beloved dead, is synonymous with the work of business. How productive; how convenient for the world's corporations.

An obvious ideology critique can be made of this story. To the surprise of absolutely nobody, Working in Business enforced ideas that support capitalist practices. My course suggested that the path from sadness to health is to work as though nothing had changed. This is a predictable and logical view for a capitalist to adopt as a worker's mourning is a direct attack on economic output. Grief has an opportunity cost. Capitalist logic dictates that we should not spend our time on unproductive pursuits like depression. There is always money to be made and capital to accumulate. We cannot afford to mourn.[12]

There is merit to the view that my course simply espoused capitalist propaganda. It was my original opinion of it; yet I now believe this position lacks nuance, and ultimately fails to acknowledge the complex relationship between work and mourning. Indeed, in some circumstances productive work can help us complete the work of mourning, as a moving passage from Andrew Solomon's *Noonday Demon* illustrates. At the end of his first chapter Solomon describes the therapeutic practice of a Cambodian woman named Phaly Nuon, a 'sometime candidate for the Nobel Peace Prize' [13] who dedicated her life to rehabilitating survivors of Pol Pot's brutal political regime. Nuon had little guidance and no training when she started her vital work. Remarkably though, she still managed to cultivate some highly successful techniques for treating survivors' depression, and developed a therapy consisting of three essential steps. 'First,' she says, 'I teach them to forget.' Then, once 'their minds are cleared of what they have forgotten, when they have learned forgetfulness well, I teach them to work.' Lastly, after they have 'mastered work... I teach them to love.'[14] To women who have lost their partners, their children, their livelihood, their homes— in short, their world—Nuon offered forgetting, work and love as therapy. All three proved indispensable to their convalescence.

Curiously, Nuon does not see forgetting, working and loving as 'three separate skills.' To her, they are 'part of one enormous whole,' and it is 'the practice of these things together... that

---

[12] This view of mourning also contains traces of a deeper capitalist notion: that action is better than accidie. It implies that productivity and a frenetic schedule rather than rest and reflection are the signs of a healthy psyche. Today this is a common belief, and it flows directly from our neoliberal culture of self-actualisation and achievement.

[13] *The Noonday Demon*, p.34.

[14] Ibid, pp.36–7.

makes a difference.'[15] Neither Nuon nor Solomon specify what they mean by this 'one enormous whole,' nor do they explain exactly what kind of 'difference' it makes. But given our earlier discussion, I believe that the 'whole' is nothing other than Freud's work of mourning. As we saw, mourning is a creative and positive process that replaces absence with symbolic knowledge. Loving and forgetting have an obvious role in such a process: to love again after a loss displaces the lost object with something new, while forgetting moves the lost object into the mind's shadows, turning a lingering image into absence. Working is equally important. Work can give us sensory stimulus that displaces other thoughts in our mind, allowing us to forget; and if we begin an original creative task, we can love and care for a project while transmuting our loss into a physical thing outside the conscious mind. All Nuon's techniques, then, are positive, creative acts that allow us to complete the work of mourning. They all help us lose our beloved object on the psychic level, leaving liberty and openness in its place; each act can fill the void with presence.

If Nuon's process displaces what is lost with the new, we can say that her techniques literally 'make a difference' in the psyche. Loving, forgetting and working create change in our minds; in a general sense, they all create a difference where a lost object once was. Elaborating this, it seems that when we undertake the work of mourning, difference is precisely what we aim to create; healthy grieving creates difference within us.

The work of mourning gives us difference; is it any surprise, then, that indifference is a defining feature of frustrated mourning, of melancholia? Or that depressed people are often unable to complete creative works? If a successful work of mourning involves the production of difference, then melancholia, its opposite, needs us to produce the opposite of difference. To preserve their lost object, the melancholic tries to ensure their lost object remains unchanged, not-different or indifferent in their mind. As such, the depressed person finds loving, working and forgetting impossible, for each act would

---

[15] Ibid.

introduce difference into a mind that desperately seeks indifference.[16] The 'work of melancholia', as Freud put it,[17] is the production of indifference.

If Nuon is correct, then work can make a difference in our minds; it can act as an antidepressant, counteract melancholia and progress the work of mourning. Despite this, there is a certain danger in work for the mourner. Though it can produce the difference necessary for mourning, it can also contribute to an aggrieved persons' program of indifference. It can do so by preserving or enabling identification: if our work habits are built on an identification with our parents' wishes or demands, work can be a means of maintaining that identification when the

---

[16] For an example of depressive indifference it is hard to surpass Camus' *L'Etranger*. After losing his mother, Meursault displays a startling lack of emotion. His apathy at her funeral and in the ensuing days is part of a program of indifference that eventually leads Meursault to commit a senseless murder, for which he is condemned to death. While Camus presents Meursault's indifference as a philosophical problem, an example of the 'Absurd' attitude, there are clues in the text that suggest that it may be more psychological in nature. Meursault has a uniquely traumatic past. At the book's end, we learn that Meursault 'never knew' his father, and knows but one story about the man (p.110). Earlier, we also learn that Meursault wasn't always indifferent to his fate. As a student, he 'had lots of ambitions' to live abroad, travel and excel at his work. But before he finished his education he 'had to' give up his studies and get a job, an event that lead to his nihilistic indifference. 'When I had to give up my studies,' he says, 'I learned very quickly that none if it really mattered' (p.41). While this statement gives a glimpse of the birth of Meursault's apathy, the abandonment of his education is never explained or referred to again. Much like his father's absence, why he 'had to' stop remains obscure. While neither of these clues are conclusive about the source of his indifference, they do suggest that his apathy may have emerged as a melancholic response to loss rather than a process of rational, philosophical deliberation.

[17] 'Mourning and Melancholia,' in the *Future of an Illusion*, p.90.

parents have been lost. Likewise, a person who negatively identifies with their parents may sublimate their hatred in an ambitious pursuit; work, then, will preserve this sublimation in the event of the loss, allowing them to avoid facing the guilt and hatred underlying their actions. But besides identification and sublimation, work can also produce indifference through a simpler mechanism: time. To the mourning process we must give our attention and care; we must give it our time, in a word. Hours and days are needed to produce the words, the language, the judgement needed to articulate loss. Making a difference in mourning needs time and failing to give time to mourning can frustrate the process. But the commitments of work demand these same resources from us: to our employers we also give our attention, care and time. There is a kind of economic competition between work and mourning: both compete for our scarce resources, for time that is irretrievably lost once spent.

The social injunction to work represses our need to mourn, and the worker confronted by the need to mourn must make a trade-off. The morning of work demands that he continue his production, working efficiently as though nothing had changed. It calls him to repress his loss with his productivity. At the same time, the work of mourning demands that he take as much time as he needs to create his loss. The former asks that he produce economic output and indifference with his precious resources, while the latter asks him to take time to produce difference. What he chooses will inevitably reflect his values—whether he cares more for efficiency that represses grief and risks melancholia or for a completed mourning that risks economic output.

Work can either aid or inhibit mourning; thus, the connection between work and mourning is deeply ambivalent. It is impossible to say whether a mourner's work will produce difference or indifference, for it is not work itself that is at issue but the function of the work for the particular mourner. Nonetheless we should be wary of our culture wherein the injunction to work productively has become absolute and where technology has given every moment of our life an economic opportunity cost.[18] Irrespective of their needs, most people in mourning cannot afford to take the time they need to complete the work of mourning. Whether or not they are especially vulnerable to melancholia, their labour contract ensures that the time they can spare on mourning is limited. Come the morning of work, people are pressed to neglect the work of mourning. Their mourning can be blocked simply because they lack time to grieve.

Regarding mourning, our culture's great crime is our lack of respect for our individual need for time. Some people need time to mourn; unfortunately not everyone can have it. Melancholic sadness can only proliferate in the wake of this neglect.

V
Love Dog

The demands of our world. Who hasn't failed the work of mourning?

I, too, am guilty.

Years ago I abandoned my beloved dog to go to college in another city. Lonely little love dog. I needed to learn how to Work in Business. This was important.

When I left home I kissed him on the head like it was our last moment together. A kind of love anxiety: his death would come, each day sooner and sooner, and I couldn't know when. Treasure each second like it was terminal. The scarcity of our moments; the impossible value of time constantly lost forever. Love slips endlessly into the past.

---

[18] I.e., whenever we have a free moment, we can instantaneously trade stocks, buy cryptocurrency, work for Uber, cultivate and promote our online presence on social media...

In my fear, sometimes I hoped to go first. That way I wouldn't lose him. What burden, grief.

A few years after we lost one another to distance, my dog died. My parents had to put him down. A call in the morning from my father's office brought the news. My dog had broken his leg. At his age, an untreatable injury.

Before the vet arrived at our house in the late afternoon, I saw my dog for a final time over a video call. Last seconds. A desperate need to believe he felt me there. But what words could I say? I consciously treasured the moment, a desperate mnemonic grip on time. I said my goodbyes hoping he understood. Then the call ended. In my hand I held a black-screened phone and I found myself in a savage silence. It was the quietude of raw loss, the void before the fury of tears. Death in the present moment, demanding I speak. But what words could I say?

As I wept in my distant city, my mother watched as the vet lifted his golden body down our front steps, the nacreous refraction of dying light anointing the air, tangerine, peach, blood orange and aureate, our love's spirit dissipating in the sky above the twinkling city lights. My dog died in the afternoon. The next morning I returned to work.

At this final departure, but also in all those that came before, a need for the work of mourning arose. To leave I had to lose my dog. But each time I was busy—wasn't I? What hours were there for tears, for an unproductive cry, when all the world's work had to be done? Come the morning of work it couldn't be justified.

But beyond the demands of work there was a quiet akin to cowardice. To my love dog what words could I say? I had no idea. Instead of thinking with creativity and bravery I chose silence, a grief gravid with the weight of the void. The urge to speak but with nothing to say. So I tried to move on, lacking the language I needed to lose him, his spirit limping at the edge of my mind.

The work of mourning always exceeds us for we do not know the meaning of loss until it arrives. Maybe we never really know it; always we can only try and meet it with courage and poetry. Maybe we fail; we are only human, but at least the attempt respects our need to speak with death, to complete that dialogue with the unknown that makes a difference, that gives us peace. Oh, had I known that then.

VI
Provoking Loss

Between these stories we can see a certain ethic of loss, a strange logic of feeling. People today trade the work of mourning for the morning of work; doing so, they suspend their sadness and slip into indifference. While they remain productive they risk depression; the opportunity cost for their work is their happiness and their investment in the world.

We have now seen how work can frustrate mourning and produce indifference, but we haven't yet understood how work functions as a cause of mourning and provokes loss. To do so, we will turn to Andrew Solomon's 'Atlas of Depression' *The Noonday Demon*, a classic work that covers everything from the treatment of the illness to the history of the concept and the political factors that exacerbate, mediate and ameliorate our experience of it.

Throughout *The Noonday Demon* Solomon discusses the complexities of post-industrial life that exacerbate our depression; among other factors, he blames the pace and chaos of our lives; the alienation and anomie that comes with industrial production; and the loneliness and purposelessness coming from the collapse of traditional social, religious, and political structures, along with our systems of belief.[19] Elsewhere, he says depression can come from the chronic stress that can occur when we 'take on jobs that [we] regret,'[20] or when we participate in 'twenty-

---

[19]   *The Noonday Demon*, pp.32, 314 & 321.
[20]   Ibid, p.407.

first century nomadism,' relocating and resettling to accommodate these jobs we might eventually lament.[21]

Chaos, change and stress, all of which can stem from our employment, are factors that can worsen our depression. Building upon this, Solomon also writes that life events themselves 'are often the triggers' for depression. He says these life events 'typically involve loss—of a valued person, of a role, of an idea about yourself'—and are worst when they involve humiliation or a sense of being trapped. But he also notes that depression can result from positive changes: 'having a baby, getting a promotion or getting married are almost as likely to kindle depression as a death or loss,' he says.[22] In this vein he also argues that depression is 'often a sign that [your] resources are being poorly invested and need to be refocused;'[23] that is, depression can force us to abandon pursuits that have wasted our energies, encouraging us to devote our attention to more pressing matters.

Four themes unite Solomon's statements: depression, social change, loss and work. Whether his writing concerns the loss of identity, social connection, spirituality or alternative opportunities for living—be they jobs we might prefer or pursuits that better suit us—Solomon continually alludes to people displaced and bereaved by changes they cannot control. Each quote depicts an individual loss that can be connected to social upheaval. Modern society in his eyes is a place increasingly beset by loss. At the same time its relentless pace, unending chaos and escalating demands for change are the sources of these losses.

Reading Solomon, we get the sense we live in a contradictory time. Modernity has increased our prosperity and our possibilities; counterbalancing this is an ever-growing abyss of loss. Opportunity cost has grown with opportunity and loss has risen with gain: this is the implication of his arguments. If we combine Solomon's insights about modern loss with those from psychoanalytic theory, then we must infer that the need to mourn

---

[21] Ibid, p.408.
[22] Ibid, p.62.
[23] Ibid, p.409.

has increased too. Where a loss has occurred humans will naturally confront the need to complete the work of mourning. When the degree of loss increases for society then the time spent mourning must also rise. Alternatively, our mourning must become more efficient or we must become less sensitive to keep pace with our losses. Failing an increase in time or efficiency we will lack the resources needed to complete the work of mourning. Our need to mourn will be frustrated; the work will remain incomplete.

In modern society the lack of time is a barrier to mourning. Time-poor on the morning of work, our social and economic obligations place pressure on the work of mourning. We workers of the world are told to continue life, to sacrifice as little as possible to the work of mourning. We are told to carry on. With our mourning blocked by this demand, psychoanalytic theory suggests that we risk falling into melancholia. Overwhelmed by a need to mourn that we have denied, we fall into apathetic lethargy. Rather than producing and welcoming difference, or spending time overcoming our identification with our lost beloved, we neglect or repress our loss and become numb, anhedonic and indifferent to change.

If my deductions are correct—this assumes nothing more than the accuracy of both Solomon's information and the arguments of psychoanalytic theory—then the injunction to work in our society is a cause of depression. Structurally speaking our society tends towards a state where the need to mourn outweighs our ability to do so: where, through an excess of loss and a shortage of time, mourning is frustrated and blocked. Our rising rates of depression are the logical consequence of this arrangement which promotes numbness and melancholia.

The industrial colonisation of the day's hours—of the morning of work—has become a block to mourning and a possible cause of depression. More and more we do not—or rather, cannot—spare the time for mourning; for the sake of our social obligations we risk giving ourselves to melancholia. And being a species of activity that demands sacrifice, upheaval and loss for the sake of economic gain, work materially contributes to this arrangement.

Once we finish school, we are encouraged to leave our homes, families and towns for college. When we graduate with our degrees, we are told to abandon our friends and campuses for other cities. Once there, surrounded by tenuous connections, we will abscond further if the opportunity arises, pursuing our ambitions to the edge of the earth. If we are successful, each movement can provide us with a measurable gain. But these changes, alongside the opportunity cost of the work itself as measured in hours of love, rest, joy and connection, also laden our hearts with an immeasurable loss: we are haunted by all the possible futures we foreclosed, the pasts that never had a chance to live. A commitment to work produces a simultaneous need for mourning, yet it is the time required by that commitment that makes proper mourning difficult.

Work, the source of our wealth and fount of our losses, leaves us too time-poor for the work of mourning it provokes. To rise on the morning of work and choose the work of mourning: does anyone have the time for that? Only if they sacrifice their economic productivity to attend to the work demanded by their loss. But can we afford that loss? Are we brave enough to choose the irrational and complete the work of mourning at the expense of our work? Are we so free to respect the dead? To give them our time and receive a language of loss in exchange? Can we allow ourselves to lose their love? If not, are we prepared to risk numbness and depression? At what cost does all of this come? How can we ever be rational when we speak of those lost and gone?

VII
[untitled, wordless]

My father once gave me some career advice; he said I should always 'go where the job takes you.' He and his friends had followed this ethic themselves and it served them well. Years ago his medical career called him from his hometown into the world and he never returned. Obliging the brutal commitments of medical school and the hospital he moved between cities and countries, eventually settling where he knew nobody. We, his family, were all he had.

My father gained much over his career; he also lost much along the way. But unlike me he had no need to study Working in Business. He already knew he had to throw himself into work to deal with loss. Somewhere he had learned the self-reinforcing magic formula for productivity and emotional intelligence: sacrifice everything for work, and when the loss becomes unbearable, work even more. He knew that repression and sublimation are the secrets to success.

Working relentlessly no matter what, my father understood work's power: he let economic devotion smother his feelings of loss. For a time kept the sadness at bay. Being busy, there was no room for mourning, but when work was quiet or when he was forced into rest, his sadness, transmuted by repression into wordless anger and an undirected sense of injustice, would occasionally break out. We would glimpse a quaking fury shaking beneath the flurry of activity. Aside from these volcanic moments though there were no signs anything was wrong. For years my father kept on working.

His attempt to choose work over mourning was undoubtedly powerful. Nonetheless my father is human. Unlike the hypothetical Worker in Business, the numbness that necessarily grew in severity as his anger and sadness festered gradually consumed him. First my father was quietly and unspeakably devastated by his mother's departure. Eventually he was adrift in an inarticulate and oceanic sadness. Depressed. And for the love of God, he had no idea why. If only this man, this doctor of life, this shield against death, had given himself the time for loss. Maybe he would have found the language to signify the open wound in his heart and create the words he needed to heal; maybe he could have reforged his identity anew in the wake of this unbearable loss. Instead he was speechless, wordless. And in silence an untitled and unnamed sadness filled his heart; it brims with it today, and our home is filled with the clamour of failed words.

VIII
The Politics of Mourning

Human loss; that mammal sadness. Our condition, we know, is a tragedy. We depend endlessly on others who will perish and our love is condemned to seek the ephemeral. To live without loss—to move through our world and encounter neither poverty nor grief but only bounty and plenty—this is a dream of days unknown to us. We lose and lose, so it's our fate to be mournful creatures; animals who, thrust into the light, begin their slip into dark without delay.

In such grief how is life anything but despair? The pain of a moment, a year—both are infinities the heart can hardly bear. Our sadness must be contained and words, all told, are our only defence. In language, unspeakable loss becomes poetry and pain fades into history. Words signify our losses; strangely, the materials of memory help us forget.[24]

Everybody in our world must experience loss but only some fall victim to depression; some succumb to this malady due to the clash between the injunction to work and the more universal need to mourn. Our societies' laws and norms create a degree of

---

[24] Here I think of a passage from p.543 of Don DeLillo's *Underworld*, where a character who wants to transcend the traumas of his past realises the importance of language. 'I wanted to look up words,' he says, 'and memorise the fuckers for all time, spell them, learn them, pronounce them syllable by syllable... This is the only way in the world you can escape the things that made you.'

competition between work and mourning: come the morning of work, we cannot mourn freely. Our grief and depression are originally personal, familial and communal acts that have been made political by the rules around work.

If our society seriously aims to relieve unnecessary depression, we should reconsider our relationship to work and mourning. To prevent avoidable melancholic depression—and to reduce the economic inefficiencies that result from it—we must minimise the competition between work and mourning. We must improve the politics of mourning that reign today; this means we must reform the politics of work that lead labour and grief to compete.

To improve our politics of mourning, we must learn to respect the course of loss. Mourning is a primary psychological need for the aggrieved; this means they need the freedom to mourn. With all our generosity and compassion, we should help them complete this work safely and thoroughly, and we should remove things that frustrate or block this vital work. As Phaly Nuon found in her work with the Cambodian refugees, we need time for labour that helps us love and forget. To reform our politics of mourning, then, we need work that contains love, that is love, that is united with love: only this can shield us against melancholia.

So far as love, work and mourning are inextricable, our new politics of mourning and work must also be a politics of love. In a way, the work of love mirrors that of mourning. To love someone, we must know and accept them intimately. [25] Yet because our lover's future is unknowable and our perceptions are distorted and partial, the knowledge created in love is contingent, and must be refreshed and recreated constantly. Our

---

[25]   Intimacy, love and knowledge are inseparable. The etymology of the word 'intimate' suggests this point. 'Intimate' is derived from the Latin *intimare* meaning 'to make known, impress, announce.' To be loved, or to be intimate with another, we must make ourselves known to that other; conversely, the other must receive this and come to know us themselves. While love is not entirely reducible to knowledge, the latter is a necessary condition of it.

understanding of our beloved must also contain a recognition of its insufficiency; it must be an enlightened ignorance, a knowledge that accepts its limits.

In loving, then, we must see the other as a fount of difference, gains, and losses, as a figure that affirms the fact of change through time. For this reason, the work of love is like the work of mourning: both use creativity to embrace the difference, the grief, the possibilities, brought forth by the motion of time. And melancholic depression is both a temporal disease and an epistemic disaster: by denying change and plunging us into indifference, depression blunts the tragedy of time.

When we speak of loving work, we refer to work that embraces the tragedies of mourning and love; loving work sees that love and mourning are forever intertwined, and like them, it creates and accepts difference.[26] It is not for me to say what kinds of work allow us to love or mourn or welcome difference; the needed difference is different for us all. For some, writing essays to help their loved ones may be enough; for others, an extended leave of absence, a retreat into quietude and isolation or a journey away from home may be needed; for others still, the steadiness of a routine or the monotonous tasks and defined structures of their work may help them grieve. We all speak a different, idiosyncratic

---

[26] When we speak of uniting love and work, we don't mean it in the banal sense prevalent today, where people insist on loving their work even when they are subject to flagrant exploitation and abuse in their employment. Their work is often antithetical to love of any kind: sadly they debase both this word and themselves by using it this way. This form of love has an obvious ideological function. Those who love their work are more likely to work relentlessly at their job, and will do so without an expectation of payment. Too often the admission that we 'love work' masks a willingness to be exploited by those who do not love us: in short, it evinces a disturbing lack of love in the speaker. And the cultural injunction for us to 'do what we love,' despite its valid existentialist logic, is little more than a command to open ourselves to such exploitation.

language of love; when we are met with loss, then, the words we find in mourning must be just as varied and unique.

Vladimir Nabokov began his memoir by writing that 'life is but a brief crack of light between two eternities of darkness;' this, he said, was the 'common sense' view of death. At times in my life I, like so many others, have believed that death is nothingness. But the creativity inherent in mourning suggests to me that Socrates had the better view: 'Death,' he said in his *Apology*, 'may even be the greatest of all good things for a human being— no one knows, yet people fear it as if they knew for sure that it's the greatest of bad things.' If we are ignorant of death as Socrates suggests, differences in mourning not only exist because of the differences in life; they also exist because we are ignorant about the nature and meaning of death. When we lose another to death's great dissolution, we are confronted with the incomprehensible: we have no idea where the other has gone and we don't know if they have found peace. Death resists understanding; despite this, mourning asks that we create a new knowledge of the departed. In loss, we therefore confront the impossible. We can say nothing about death, yet mourning asks us to speak a maelstrom of words; death calls us to silence and in sadness we answer with a fury of language. Because death is unknown and undetermined while a knowledge of loss is necessary, the work of mourning is unpredictable and forever incomplete. In our struggle to live against restless decay we are condemned to failure. Our mourning will always fall short. But this is not an excuse for inaction, which can only lead to melancholia; rather it is an argument for free and pluralistic mourning and love, for an openness to difference that allows us to derive the unfixed, unfinished knowledge specific to each loss.

The indeterminacy of mourning ultimately gives us the structure of our politics; it is a justification for agnosticism and socialism. If we really care for others, we must work to give each other the time, resources and support we all need for mourning; we must do so precisely because we are ignorant, insufficient and imperfect; because we are creatures who must love what we cannot understand.

In our politics of mourning we cannot demand a rigid or set structure for mourning; instead, we demand a respect for our differences in grief, for a tenor of compassion that hears the cries of our hearts and allows us to break and rebuild as we need. The point is to let everyone find the right language for their loss. Our politics therefore asks for one thing: that come the morning of work we may tend to the work of mourning as we require. It also insists that this right is inseparable from the right to love; to remain open to difference, to love, we must mourn.

Freud once wrote that 'we must begin to love in order not to fall ill, and we are bound to fall ill if, in consequence of frustration, we are unable to love.'[27] We love to avoid depression, and we speak and mourn for the same reason: each act helps us find new words, however insufficient, that allow us to live in difference. Such is our only defence against the sickness of indifference, the death-in-life of melancholic depression; it is the only way we can see others and ourselves for what we are. With love in mind, we now see how we must live. Our potential for tenderness, sadness and passion redeems us and preserves our desire for life: against depression and indifference, then, let us be generous with our time and help others to crack, to heal, to love, to live as they need. And above all, for the sake of love: speak, and give your lost love the significance they deserve. For in language, in sadness, you can leave the hell of depression for the open rush of love; we can submerge ourselves in the flood of tragic beauty whose surge and recession marks nothing if not a life wholly lived.

---

[27] See *On Narcissism: An Introduction*

Selected Bibliography

Alvarez, A. (1971). *The Savage God: A Study of Suicide*. Singapore: Penguin Books.

Arendt, H. (2017). *The Origins of Totalitarianism*. Great Britain: Penguin Classics.

Banville, J. (2005). *The Sea*. London: Picador.

Beckett, S. (2009). *Three Novels: Molloy, Malone Dies, The Unnamable*. New York, NY: Grove Press.

Camus, A. (1989). *The Stranger*. Vintage International.

Camus, A. (2013). *The Rebel*. Great Britain: Penguin Classics.

Caputo, J. D. (2018). *Hermeneutics: Facts and Interpretation in the Age of Information*. Great Britain: Pelican Books.

Chomsky, N. (1966). *Cartesian Linguistics: A Chapter in the History of Rationalist Thought*. New York, NY: Harper & Row.

Chomsky, N., & Waterstone, M. (2021). *Consequences of Capitalism: Manufacturing Discontent and Resistance*. Great Britain: Hamish Hamilton.

Deleuze, G. (1994). *Difference & Repetition*. New York, NY: Columbia University Press.

DeLillo, D. (1992). *Mao II*. Great Britain: Vintage.

DeLillo, D. (1998). *Underworld*. Great Britain: Picador.

DeLillo, D. (2011). *Libra*. London: Penguin Group.

Foucault, M. (1995). *Discipline & Punish*. New York, NY: Random House.

Freud, S. (2004). *The Future of an Illusion*. London: Penguin Group.

Freud, S. (1914). *On Narcissism: An Introduction*. Retrieved from https://www.sakkyndig.com/psykologi/artvit/freud1925.pdf

Guntrip, H. (1969). *Schizoid Phenomena, Object Relations & The Self*. NY: International Universities Press, Inc.

Heidegger, M. (1977). *The Question Concerning Technology & Other Essays*. New York, NY: Garland Publishing Inc.

Heidegger, M. (2010). *Being & Time*. Albany, NY: State University of New York Press.

Leader, D. (2008). *The New Black: Mourning, Melancholia & Depression*. London, UK: Penguin Group.

Nabokov, V. (2008). *Lolita*. Australia: Penguin Group.

Nabokov, V. (2011). *Pale Fire*. London: Penguin Group.

Nietzsche, F. (2018). *The Joyous Science*. Great Britain: Penguin Classics.

Plath, S. (2013). *The Bell Jar*. UK: Faber Paperback.

Plato. (2010). *The Last Days of Socrates*. England: Penguin Group.

Sartre, J. P. (1965). *Nausea*. Great Britain: Penguin Group.

Savery, D. (2018). *Echoism: The Silenced Response to Narcissism*. Routledge.

Shaw, D. (2014). *Traumatic Narcissism: Relational Systems of Subjugation*. New York, NY: Routledge.

Solomon, A. (2001). *The Noonday Demon: An Anatomy of Depression*. London: Vintage.

Sontag, S. (2001). *Against Interpretation and Other Essays*. Picador.

Varoufakis, Y. (2017). *Adults in the Room: My Battle With Europe's Deep Establishment*. London: Vintage.

Wallace, D. F. (1997). *Infinite Jest*. USA: Abacus.

Wallace, D. F. (2005). *Consider the Lobster*. Great Britain: Abacus.

Wallace, D. F. (2012). *Both Flesh & Not*. Australia: Penguin Group.

Žižek, S. (2002). *Welcome to the Desert of the Real! Five Essays on September 11 and Related Dates*. London: Verso.

Žižek, S. (2008). *The Sublime Object of Ideology*. London: Verso.

Žižek, S. (2020). *Sex and the Failed Absolute*. UK: Bloomsbury Academic.

Acknowledgments

I owe a special debt to a few people without whom this book would not exist.

First, thank you to Lucas Smith, Andrea Jonathan, and the rest of the team at Bonfire Books. New writers depend on publishers like Bonfire—publishers who are prepared to take risks for literature and support emerging talent. You have a rare and admirable faith in new (and old) Australian literature, and you were the first to take a chance on me and my writing. For that I am forever grateful.

Now, my family. A special thanks to my Mum for always being the first and most enthusiastic of my readers, and to my Dad for so graciously consenting to his portrayal in the final essay. Thanks also to my Uncle Nick, whose demand for essays on economics indirectly led me to write this book. And love and thanks, of course, to my siblings and friends, Hamish, Sam, and Laura.

My dearest thanks to Ben, my oldest friend, whose unwavering belief in me and my writing sustains me. Your support, aesthetic and otherwise, was indispensable as I began my writing life.

G. G. – your empathy and 'evenly-suspended attention' over the last years have been so important for the growth of my life and art. Without you my speech would not be nearly so free. Thank you for everything.

Many of my friends read early versions of these essays, or endured rehearsals of my arguments in verbal form. Nick, Jacob, Bridie, Jamie, Harriet, Sam, Emily, Joe, Lizzie, Jen, Mike, Nestor, and everyone else: your support and interest were much appreciated.

Sam Cooney read and edited the first (and much, much longer) draft of this book. His guidance in this stage and beyond was invaluable, and I thank him for his help. Yanis Varoufakis read this book's proof in March 2022, and provided the lovely and eloquent quote used on the back cover. His support was beyond generous, and to him, I say: thank you, and *carpe DiEM.*

My former boss motivated the dialectic of negation that made me a full-time writer. Misery must eventually become its opposite, and I thank her for inaugurating that process.

The A. D. C. Fund for Impoverished Writers provided economic stimulus during the editing stage of this book, for which I am grateful. The book in your hands is proof positive of the multiplier effect of fiscal generosity.

Finally, my love and gratitude to my partner, Nicola. Your talents for joy and warmth and care are vital to me; your spirit lingers among all the words of this book.